THE RISE AND FALL OF BRITISH RAILWAYS

GOODS
& FREIGHT

JOHN VAUGHAN

Haynes Publishing

First published in 2012 by Haynes Publishing

A catalogue record for this book is available from the British Library.

ISBN 978 0 85733 023 9

Library of Congress control no. 2011935263

Published by Haynes Publishing,
Sparkford, Yeovil, Somerset BA22 7JJ, UK

Tel: 01963 442030 Fax: 01963 440001

Int. tel: +44 1963 442030 Int. fax: +44 1963 440001

E-mail: sales@haynes.co.uk

Website: www.haynes.co.uk

Haynes North America Inc., 861 Lawrence Drive,
Newbury Park, California 91320, USA

Printed in the USA by Odcombe Press LP,
1299 Bridgestone Parkway, La Vergne, TN 37086

Page 1: The dying embers of a generation, some might say an entire age, are about to be extinguished in this late 1965 view as the last month of steam traction on the Western Region of British Railways (BR) approaches. Giving its all as it heads south from Oxford, 'Hall' class 4-6-0 No 6956 *Mottram Hall* in filthy, nameless and numberless condition and with steam leaks a-plenty, makes for Didcot on a cold frosty morning with a typical mixed freight of the era. *Author*

Page 2: A photograph that encapsulates the fundamental problem of the freight scene on British Railways both pre- and post-Beeching; lightly loaded goods trains and wagonload freight workings that cost considerably more to operate than the income derived from the customer source. One of the dual-traction Class 73s, here operating in electric mode on a 750V dc third-rail system, heads just a wagon of concrete sleepers and two HEA wagons of coal through Bosham while working from Fratton yard to Brighton (goods) via Chichester in 1983, hence the '1B' headcode. The scene is further dated by the upper quadrant semaphore signal. *Author*

Page 3: A wonderful impression of a good old-fashioned goods and marshalling yard, photographed at Rose Grove on 18 April 1968, just weeks before standard gauge steam ended on BR. Shunting the yard is 8F 2-8-0 No 48167, its number simply too dirty to read, while 'Black Five' 4-6-0 No 45397 heads eastbound for Copy Pit with a rake of empty coal wagons. The variety of fitted and unfitted wooden and metal-bodied wagons is remarkable, with perhaps the highly inflammable 'Benzene' wagon being the focal point. Every track in this scene except the main running lines has been swept away in the name of progress. *Author*

Opposite: For many decades, British Railways used horses to shunt wagons at certain locations and research reveals that the last two locations where such operations could be observed were at Hayle in Cornwall and, appropriately, Newmarket in Cambridgeshire. Here, a double-headed horse working is seen on Hayle Wharves on lines long since abandoned. *Author's collection*

CONTENTS

INTRODUCTION

WELCOME TO THE THIRD BOOK in a trilogy that describes in words and pictures 'The Rise and Fall of British Railways' between the years 1948 and 1997. There is a brief mention of the pre-Nationalisation period, and the transition from British Rail's business sectors to rail privatisation. Earlier volumes dealt with 'Main Line Diesel Locomotives' and 'Branches and Minor Lines', whereas this volume deals with 'Goods and Freight' trains and traffic.

The conveyance of goods and freight by rail has an interesting history. There has of course always been a need for an immense variety of commercial consignments to be moved from place to place, but with the coming of the industrial revolution in Victorian times, the movement of sometimes heavy loads became necessary over longer and longer distances. Canals had their place in fulfilling this requirement, but the need for locks in order to gain or lose height and the primary use of horse power resulted in very slow average speeds. Also, there were vast areas of the UK that were not canal served resulting in considerable trans-shipment from canal terminals or basins to horse-drawn wagons that were obliged to use primitive roads and tracks.

There had been tramways at some industrial sites for many years prior to the 1830 opening of public railways but after that date the railway wagon soon became the prime vehicle for the transportation of goods. By 1850, just over 20 years after the opening of the Liverpool & Manchester Railway, the income from freight traffic on our railways exceeded passenger receipts. By 1870, for every £2 received from selling tickets to passengers £3 was received from goods and freight traffic. As a matter of interest a century later, in 1970, the two prime sources of rail traffic were about equal, but by 1980 the position compared with 1870 was reversed with income from passenger services being twice that received from freight.

Our railways gradually developed through the late Victorian era when the only practical transport alternatives were inland waterways, horse and cart, or coastal sailing vessels. In addition to main lines, branches and minor lines spawned, but the advent of the motor car and motor lorry was rapidly approaching. With the deficiencies of horse transport and poor roads the railways held a virtual monopoly in many areas, with the exception of remote villages and hamlets that were without access to rail transport, but the imminent threat of motorised transport, which had the potential to serve every area of the country on a door-to-door basis, was a very different proposition that would soon challenge that monopoly.

In many areas with significant populations stations were located every few miles. Most of these stations had adjacent goods yards, which were used by merchants for an infinite range of freight items, ranging from agricultural produce to coal and oil, and from livestock to manufactured goods. This required an enormous fleet of wagons to satisfy the huge demand, especially as many consignments comprised a single wagonload or less. Collection and delivery services also had to be provided. All of this action resulted in a remarkable diversity of wagon movements. The smooth working of complete trains was inevitably hampered by the shunting of hundreds of thousands of wagons destined for a vast number of loading and unloading points throughout the nation. The staging of wagons from marshalling yard to marshalling yard and from siding to siding before delivery to local customers was complex, time-consuming and inefficient, with variable and cumulative delays leading to slow and unpredictable journey times.

Another major problem, especially in terms of modernisation and the procurement of new wagons, was that because of their potential nationwide movement, all of these wagons had to be compatible in terms of coupling and where appropriate, braking systems. Consequently the evolution of new goods and freight rolling stock was necessarily protracted. Notwithstanding these general problems, in order to provide a comprehensive rail service countrywide, in accordance with their legal obligations as a 'common carrier', there had to be a collection and delivery service for minor consignments, which the railways were really not suited to. In providing such a service the railways abandoned their main advantage of carrying heavy loads over long distances, so successfully applied in the USA in recent decades. Thus the railways were saddled with the costly business of moving wagons in small numbers over branches and minor lines where there were too few wagons moving quickly enough to make up commercially viable freight trains. Vast sums of money were lost in such operations, which damaged the reputation of the railways.

Upon Nationalisation in 1948, BR inherited well over one million goods wagons, with all of their movements based on a paper-driven system, decades before computers were in widespread commercial use! As explained within the general text that follows, the goods and freight motive power scene was also fairly discouraging for the newly formed British Railways (BR). In many areas freight was in the hands of wheezing 50-year-old steam locomotives that had not seen major works attention for a decade or more.

There were of course some younger and quite efficient steam locomotive types within the BR freight locomotive fleet, but when combined with an ancient infrastructure, primitive small-capacity wagons (thousands without even vacuum brakes), and a creaking paper-driven administrative system there was little for the British Transport Commission (BTC) to be positive about. One of the great problems was that even if they had modernised the total freight system they would have had to have persuaded their customers to spend significant sums of money on modernisation, for example installing new wagon-loading systems at their various works, and procuring and generally handling new-build freight rolling stock, and thereby running the risk of non-compatibility with older wagons.

After years of reducing the immense backlog of railway maintenance that had occurred during the Second World War, it was to be the mid-1950s before a much-needed Modernisation Plan would herald significant change. The main content of the plan as it pertained to goods and freight is described in the next chapter, suffice to say that even though there were new wagon procurements, on the whole, the most significant change was the fitting of vacuum brakes and the gradual abandonment of wooden-body structures. Gradually, dieselisation took place but the process took nearly two decades to implement, steam finally being eliminated from the BR standard gauge network during 1968.

After Nationalisation in 1948 the railways continued to lose money and they had to be supported by the taxpayer, who was required to have deeper and deeper pockets. The above-mentioned Modernisation Plan in 1954/55 failed to stem these losses and in 1962 the government imported an industrialist to head the new British Railways Board. The objective was to identify waste and inefficiency in order to reduce losses and make the railways subsidy free. The nominated postholder was Dr Richard Beeching. There was nothing pleasing to the railway romantic in the statistics unearthed by Beeching and his team. The average turn-round time for a typical wagon, as measured from the time it was unloaded in a yard, depot or siding to the time any back load was loaded and despatched, was a staggering 11.9 working days. The average loaded transit time was between 1.5 and 2 days for a standard journey length of just 67 miles. These figures were rightly described as 'totally unacceptable'. If these figures could have been reduced to a day for loading, an absolute maximum of two days in transit and two days to unload and reload, with a consequent total turn-round time of say five days, over 500,000 fewer wagons would have been required by BR!

▼ In the pre-1923 'Grouping' era both private commercial owner wagons and those belonging to the main railway companies had their names emblazoned on the bodysides, which not only provided free publicity but also helped with identification in goods and marshalling yards. In this delightful scene at Llanymynych graceful Cambrian Railways 4-4-0 No 70 enters the station and passes a southbound goods train. Second left is a seven-plank wagon belonging to Glebe Colliery at Fenton, east of Stoke-on-Trent, and in front of that is a two-plank open wagon owned by Cambrian Railways, as well as some heavily limed cattle wagons. *SLS*

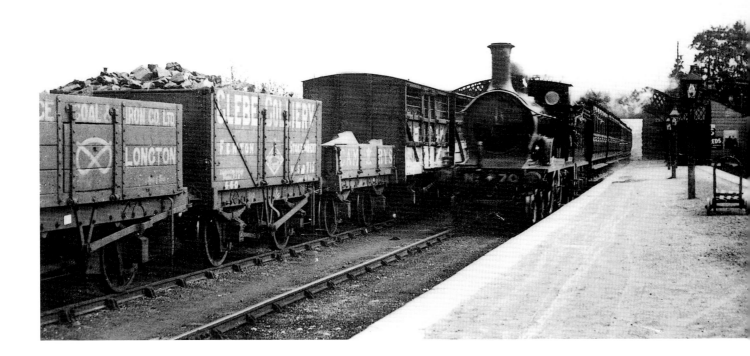

What was becoming alarming was that compared with the 11.9 days turn-round time for rail wagons, road hauliers could deliver the goods over the same distance in a single day with the lorry returning to base ready to haul another load the next day. The only viable solution to the obvious problem was to close a substantial part of the loss-making goods and freight network (and incidentally many passenger lines and services) and to develop brand-new services, over longer distances with heavier payloads, using new, larger fit-for-purpose wagons. Goods and freight by rail was in serious decline as costs increased, services became less reliable, our road systems improved, and the size of lorries increased. Also, regular industrial disputes on the railway resulted in many customers understandably abandoning freight by rail to remove the risk of militant unions impacting their businesses by causing costly delays. Many companies refused to be held to ransom or to run the risk of upsetting their customers, a luxury not afforded to the poor old entrapped commuters in the 1970s and 1980s 'Buckton' years.

Gradually much of the freight traffic pattern changed with an increasing emphasis on the block load. Many branches and minor lines were closed, wagonload pick-up goods decreased in number, a vast array of marshalling yards and smaller depots were either underutilised or had disappeared from the railway map altogether. This radical change in operations resulted in a huge number of brand-new low-powered diesel locomotives becoming redundant almost before they left the production line. However, all was not doom and gloom and there were to be some highly successful innovations, particularly merry-go-round (mgr)

pit-to-power station operations, and the gradual increase in container traffic. Whereas the big wagon issue for many years had been no brakes versus fitted vacuum brakes, later developments saw air-braked wagons ousting vacuum-braked vehicles. Similarly, most freight locomotives were modified and fitted with a train air braking capability, and by the late 1970s, air brakes were standard on new builds.

At last customers, assisted in many cases by government grants, were modernising their operations and rapid loading and unloading systems were being introduced. Higher capacity modern bogie wagons arrived on the scene, reducing the unit costs of operating most block loads. The advent of large-scale private ownership of freight vehicles arrived, saving BR millions of pounds in procurement costs and on-going wagon maintenance overheads. A computerised wagon and stock control system known as TOPS (Total Operations Processing System) was introduced in the early 1970s, which greatly speeded up traffic and information flows compared with the old cumbersome paper-driven

▼ In this wonderful example of private owner wagons dating back to the turn of the 20th century a trio of three-plank examples belonging to North and Rose China Clay & Stone Proprietors are on display beside a Cornish clay dry, having been loaded with casks containing china clay. It would appear that each wagon contains 45 casks. These barrels will more than likely make their way to the docks at Par or Fowey for shipment. There is an absence of brakes, a 10 tons load notice and the wagons are numbered 13, 8 and 9.
English China Clays Group

system. Gradually, most of the old inefficient manual systems in our industries and docks disappeared and with them a culture of nepotism, ridiculous lines of demarcation and the crippling strikes that regularly held the nation to ransom ended. Eventually, everything from limousines to paper clips ended up in company containers and the Freightliner train was born. Average speeds increased with some freights working along main lines at 75mph. The gross all-up weight of loaded wagons steadily increased, reaching and passing the 100 tonne barrier.

Another factor that greatly impacted the freight scene was the gradual change in the various commodities hauled by rail. Every significant industry was involved, especially the domestic UK coal industry. Although coal mines had been closing for many years as seams ran out or there were geological problems, the decimation of the industry during the 1980s and 1990s, following the infamous coal miners' strike, had an enormous impact on the industry. The areas most heavily affected were South Yorkshire, Nottinghamshire and Derbyshire, South Wales and Scotland. Hundreds of mines closed not only in the face of mounting losses and political dogma, but also because increasing supplies of North Sea oil and gas affected the way that households heated their homes. However, a consolation for the railways if not the UK coal industry, was the increase in the importation of cheaper coal from as far away as Australia, which was conveyed by rail from dock, rather than pit, to power station.

Other changes involved the steel industry where repeated corporate takeover activity resulted in a downturn in the number of freight trains associated with that sector. Again, there were contractions in an effort to stem losses as the UK had to compete with the rest of the world on a playing field that was hardly even, especially in respect of labour costs, and various industry controls. The oil industry still conveyed large tonnages by rail but huge investments in pipelines gradually produced an underground network that in terms of major sites spread nationwide, greatly reducing the number of tanker trains. The introduction of large bogie wagons helped modernise the heavier trains that continued to run. The once buoyant china clay industry increased tonnages for many years but again corporate changes and company takeovers saw reductions as West Country installations were rationalised and closed, and the raw material sourced in other countries.

The modernisation of the aggregates industry, with larger wagons and the introduction of more powerful locomotives, caused a seismic shift in rail transportation practices with 'jumbo' trains operating in some places, especially between the Somerset quarries and the Capital. The four-wheeled wagon fleet was modernised with air brakes, roller bearing and disc brakes, with hopper discharge becoming the norm. Every industry using freight by rail had a unique story to tell during the BR years, ranging from automobiles to domestic waste and from nuclear traffic to Ministry of Defence trains. Although the

huge loss-making wagonload trains all but disappeared, marketing names such as 'Speedlink' and much later 'Enterprise' continued to cater for smaller loads, provided they complied with conditions and locations that suited the railway operators. Many smaller customers were simply priced out of the market with the road transport industry providing a superior, cheaper and generally faster service, obviating the trans-shipment requirement.

Although there had been a few chinks of light in the UK railfreight industry simple statistics relating to the last three decades of BR's lifespan show a sorry situation in tonnage terms. In 1967, a total 124 million tons of coal were shifted by rail, but by 1997 this figure had plummeted to 52.2 million tons, a reduction of 58 per cent. Back in 1952, it had been 172.7 million tons! In the iron and steel industry tonnages were 36 million in 1967 and 15 million in 1997, also a reduction of 58 per cent. The oil industry managed to shift 12 million tons by rail in 1967 whereas the figure had shrunk to a modest 6.1 million in 1997, a reduction of 49 per cent over 30 years.

The only bright spot within the largest industries was aggregates where 10 million tons in 1967 were converted to 11.5 million tons in 1997, an increase of 15 per cent, although before spreading goods and freight joy it should be pointed out that the industry peaked at 23.5 million tons in 1989. As regards 'grand totals', statistics speak for themselves in that from total freight traffic of 289 million tons in 1952, this had reduced to 204 million tons by 1967 and by the end of BR as we knew it in 1996/97, this figure had declined to a relative paltry 101.7 million tons, little more than a third of the figure carried 50 years earlier (albeit at a huge loss). The obvious conclusion was that because of the size and therefore distances travelled within the UK, Beeching was right in that by and large, with a few exceptions, it is only the industry-specific block load freight train that is ever going to be profitable on the former BR network.

One of the great disappointments, at least in the early years of operation, has been the Channel Tunnel. As usual in the early days of planning many major schemes, which often determine budget and timescales, traffic projections are forecast. After the sounding of trumpets and the launch ballyhoo of Channel Tunnel freight services back in 1994, by the time BR petered out in 1997 barely half of the 6 million tonne target of anticipated traffic had materialised, even though by then additional UK intermodal terminals had been opened and freight was mainly in the hands of English Welsh & Scottish Railways (EWS).

One of the key assumptions had been that major customers would run self-contained block trains from European mainland termini to UK termini and vice versa, but in total traffic volumes this never justified that supposition. Virtually no provision was made for marshalling wagons at Dollands Moor, near the English tunnel entrance, and such activities were focussed on Wembley. Also, the economics of the logistics resulted in the transportation of freight from the nearer locations in France not being viable for rail haulage in a cost/efficiency comparison with road transport, a situation not helped by the tunnel carrying, via Le Shuttle, massive lorryloads piggyback style in direct competition with the railways.

During the last decade of BR there had been a number of improvements in the freight business and all was not doom and gloom. Belatedly there were some new-generation freight locomotive procurements but, again, BR was not up to speed with outside industry and it was Foster Yeoman who bought American and reaped the dividend. BR had ordered the Class 56s and later Class 58s but especially the former were, unfortunately, not the panacea for early generation diesel replacement and the author remembers visiting Cardiff Canton and seeing pieces of Class 56 spread all over the locomotive maintenance facility. The Romanian-built examples gave additional problems, especially with build quality.

▼ Even after the 1923 Grouping the 'Big Four' railway companies retained the tradition of wagon markings. Beside the linhay of another Cornish clay drying plant is a loaded Great Western Railway (GWR) five-plank wagon and two interlopers in the shape of London Midland & Scottish Railway (LMS) four-wheeled coal wagons that are being back loaded with jute sacks of china clay or stone. The journey to their destination will be a slow one by modern standards. *Author's Collection*

The Class 58s were a cost-saving solution employing modular construction with easy component access principles, but compared with the reliability and the proven technology of the General Motors Class 59s, they were second rate. Even the last BR freight locomotives ever built, the Class 60s, had a sophisticated specification, but it took over a full calendar year for BR to accept the locomotives into their stock whereas the products from North America ran successfully immediately the box was opened, with availability figures in the mid- to high 90 per cent range. However, there was plenty of retrospective food for thought at the time these words were being written because the often denigrated Class 58s have been working very successfully in France, mainly on major infrastructure projects, and a decision was made to modify and upgrade 20 Class 60s to 'Super-60s', thereby ensuring their future for a further decade. It will be wonderfully satisfying for the average UK railfan to see these leftovers from the BR era tugging away at heavy freights in direct competition with the products of our North American cousins for years to come.

The concept of sectorisation within BR in 'quiet' readiness for possible privatisation was, in retrospect, deemed to be a success. The employment of a more commercial approach to the rail business refocussed the minds of a new generation of managers, who had significant delegated responsibilities in an effort to make their respective businesses profitable. Although allowed to run free in terms of customer relations and selling their business to the world at large there were

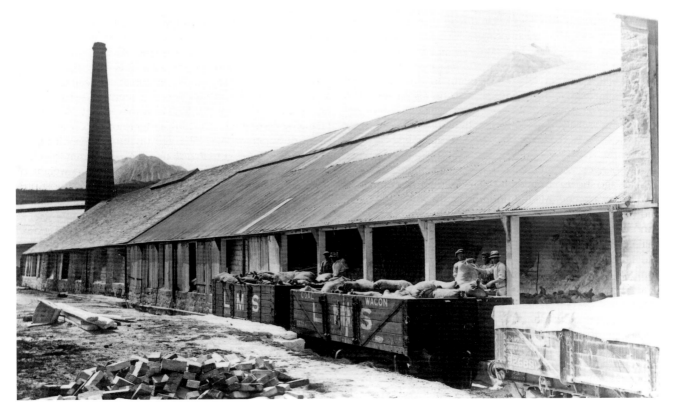

▲ There is much to observe in this view of the old West Bay terminus of the erstwhile Bridport branch line in Dorset. The station closed to passengers in September 1930 but remained open for freight until December 1962, more than 32 years! On the left is a delightful clerestory-roofed 'Camp Coach' while on the right is a long line of empty wagons showing NE (North Eastern), LMS and GW on their sides. These idle empty wagons would not be helping the goods 'turn-round' time statistics. *S.V. Blencowe*

still overall constraints, especially in the complex business of not owning important parts of the infrastructure in which they were obliged to operate, and the absorption of overheads over which the various sectors had no direct control. However, in terms of 'teeing-up' the railfreight business in readiness for privatisation the exercise served a really useful purpose. Inevitably, privatisation took much longer than anticipated and the BR freight sectors operated for a full decade in many cases.

Over the years the goods and freight scene has undergone many changes, so much so that the rail atlases of only 20 years ago show a completely different structure compared with today's scene. Many hundreds of freight lines, yards and terminals have closed, while others have changed hands. New freight-handling companies have emerged to challenge big league players like EWS (now DB Schenker) and Freightliner, while others have gone to the wall in a competitive market place. As contracts end and tenders are reissued freight companies gain and lose business. Every change and every new freight flow makes the news, as do new locomotive and wagon procurements, livery changes, freight terminal openings and closures. Some of the growth stories have been spectacular such as container traffic at the port of Felixstowe, while other loads such as liquid petroleum gas and petroleum products have declined. The good news is that since privatisation the railways' share of

national goods traffic has increased significantly, albeit from a very low baseline.

Taking the macro view over the BR years, comparing the goods and freight business in 1948 with the services provided in 1997 is almost impossible because of the amazing array of the changes in circumstance that have impacted the situation. Slowly but surely, BR did adapt to the changing commercial world both technologically and from a business perspective. The age of the old pre-Grouping steam locomotive trundling along with half a dozen wooden-bodied wagons and a brake van with an all-up weight of perhaps 180 tons seems as though it belongs to almost pre-historic times compared with a whispering Class 70 gliding along with 2,700 tonnes in tow. For the enthusiast the great reduction in the number of goods and freight trains running on the network is unfortunate, but at hotspots such as Barnetby one could be excused for thinking the railfreight business was burgeoning. Despite everything, freight traffic on the erstwhile BR network is still alive and kicking and with DB Schenker looking for a freight rail route from the UK to China via Russia, a fascinating future is assured!

John Vaughan
Goring by Sea, West Sussex
March 2012

ACKNOWLEDGEMENTS

THIS BOOK PROVIDES A BROAD OVERVIEW in both words and pictures of the fascinating goods and freight train story spanning the half-century when the erstwhile British Railways was in existence. There is also commentary and illustrations relating to the goods trains of yesteryear leading up to railway Nationalisation in 1948 as well as text and images that are post-1998 relating to the modern privatised railfreight scene. Over 360 nationwide photographs have been included showing the dramatic changes that have taken place during the past century.

The photographs have been sourced from a multiplicity of photographers and organisations and my grateful thanks for the support and cooperation that I have received is hereby acknowledged. I would particularly like to thank, in no particular order, Gavin Morrison, Brian Morrison, Michael Mensing, Anthony Guppy, John Chalcraft, Brian Lewis of the Stephenson Locomotive Society, the late W. A. 'Cam' Camwell, and all the photographers credited at the end of each caption. For general assistance my sincere gratitude goes to Peter Nicholson, Steve Davies, John Hicks, Steve Chandler, and my publishers for the freedom afforded in terms of content.

Finally, after 47 years in the railway publishing 'business' (from 1965 to 2012), and with 45 railway books 'under my belt', as well as editing 38 issues of the national *Modern Railways Pictorial* magazine between 1979 and 1983, preparing countless articles for magazines and newspapers as well as captioning many, many thousands of individual photographs for publication, not to mention running 64 enthusiasts' railtours between 1970 and 1980, I am formally retiring from the railway publishing scene to make way for a promising new generation of authors and photographers. In recent years I have worked for Haynes Publishing, Oxford Publishing Company, Ian Allan Publishing, Oakwood Press and my own Photrack imprint, but it has been very satisfying to end this secondary 'career' with a trilogy of books for the friendly folks at Haynes Publishing at Sparkford, near Yeovil.

I have had some wonderful times lineside with a camera, I have met some great people along the way and I have enjoyed writing and compiling the various publications. Thank you to all my friends and acquaintances, fellow photographers, RPPR rail tour participants, and to those who have purchased or read this and past publications that I have been privileged to author. Much personal nostalgia remains from the halcyon years and there is much I will miss in taking a step back from the railway scene, but in my view it is better to stop even a part-time 'career' from a position of strength rather than to just fade away. Enjoy the book!

◀ One of the all-time classic locomotives from the days of the small independent railway companies was the Bishop Castle Railway's 0-6-0 *Carlisle*. The original Kitson-built 0-6-0 saddle tank locomotive of 1868 vintage was later converted to an 0-6-0 tender engine and used by contractors Thomson Nelson. The line opened in 1861 and was in receivership for 69 years, finally closing in 1935 with the demolition train traversing the route in 1937. Much of the line ran beside the River Onny, which the railway crossed several times. In this atmospheric scene *Carlisle* is seen taking water from the river, 75 years ago. *W.A. Camwell/SLS*

OLD TIMERS

▶ Over the years there have been many examples of mixed train workings. Normally this applied to branch line traffic where for reasons of economy goods wagons and a passenger coach or two ran together, with leisurely stops included in the timetable to allow for shunting. However, various vans were also seen on the main line, normally for baggage and parcels. In this superb GWR scene 'Cobham' class 2-2-2 No 157, built at Swindon in 1879 with 7ft driving wheels, domed boiler and round-topped firebox, has three splendid clerestory-roofed coaches in tow as well as three assorted vans 'fore and aft'. Notice the man on the footplate leaning out of the cab with a bowler hat on! *Author's Collection*

◀ One wonders whether this train was the precursor of the modern 'Motorail', although research for a possible 'Carriagerail' service came to nothing! In this delightful scene on the GWR main line at Acton, a gleaming 4-2-2 hauls a coach on a four-wheeled flat wagon, probably belonging to a member of the aristocracy, and a single six-wheeled carriage, towards the Metropolis. It was not unusual in Victorian times for the upper classes to arrange for a private train to convey them and their personal transport between stations, especially over longer distances.
Author's Collection

▶ One of the quaintest standard gauge railways was the Selsey Tramway in what is now West Sussex. The line was part of the famous Col H.F. Stephens's railway empire and in common with the Bishop's Castle Railway it too closed in 1935. To save money the railway procured a couple of pairs of petrol railcars from the Ford and Shefflex companies but any economies failed to save the line, which succumbed to bus competition. For light goods, including milk churns, a simple wagon was often coupled between the cars. With only a couple of passengers visible the quaint ensemble passes weed-choked track beside Pagham Harbour. *Author's Collection*

▲ Most of the 'Big Four' and pre-Grouping railway companies owned large numbers of 0-6-0 steam locomotives; indeed, many locomotives of this type were called their 'standard goods engines'. They were good all-rounders, not immensely powerful but having an excellent general route availability. In this impressive view one of the LNER's workhorses leaves York with a southbound freight comprising some heavily limed cattle wagons and high-sided coal wagons. The signal gantry is nothing short of sensational. *SLS*

▼ One of the most remote branches in the UK was the Highland Railway line from Wick to Lybster in Caithness. The little-used branch that had four intermediate stations closed from 1 December 1951. In this view from April 1935 the mixed train comprised just a single coach and a horsebox, emphasising the rural nature of the location and the minimal passenger or goods traffic. The little 0-4-4T branch locomotive dates back to the McIntosh era in Victorian times and it is being looked after by the driver, with oil can in hand. *SLS*

▲ This Churchward GWR 2-6-0 Mogul has a heavy freight behind it but whatever the tonnage in tow, No 8364 will soon be working even harder as it assaults the tough climb up to Whiteball summit on the Devon/Somerset border. Storming through the now-closed Tiverton Junction station on 10 April 1935 the train has been routed via the up fast line. The remarkably mixed load will be conveying customers' wagonloads to an immense variety of destinations. Note the bold lettering on the station awning, the junction for both Tiverton Town and Hemyock. *W.A. Camwell/SLS*

▼ This rural delight shows Burwarton station on the splendidly named Cleobury Mortimer & Ditton Priors Light Railway. On 10 September 1938, a single passenger is alighting from a small, two-coach train comprising two short-wheelbase coaches, while a single goods wagon populates the single siding, which doubles as a loop. The 0-6-0PT is heading the 5.20pm from Cleobury Mortimer just a fortnight before all passenger services were withdrawn. Goods traffic continued until January 1957, although some Ministry of Defence (MoD) loads were rail hauled until 1965. *E. Hannen/SLS*

1940s AND NATIONALISATION

ALTHOUGH IT COULD BE ARGUED that the Nationalisation of Britain's railways in 1948 was a political act it is unlikely that the appalling state of our railways after many years of government control during wartime could have been rectified by the 'Big Four' railway companies, the Great Western Railway, the Southern Railway, the London Midland & Scottish Railway, and the London & North Eastern Railway, plus a handful of surviving minor independent railways and a few joint lines. After six years of war where national survival was the common cause the 'old order' of shining named expresses and fiercely independent profit-making companies paying dividends to its shareholders with a proud and loyal workforce had long disappeared, even if memories had not. The Railway Executive recognised the latter by declaring its support for the survival of individual enterprise and loyalty, hoping it would flourish in a Nationalised industry commenting that 'proud regiments are the foundation of a great army'.

During the Second World War it had not only been bomb damage to the railway infrastructure that had caused problems, but with the understandable focus on the manufacture of munitions and armaments combined with restrictions on non-military manufacturing and a shortage of raw materials, there had been precious little replacement of worn-out machinery on our railways, whether point rods and track, or locomotives and rolling stock. Except for the building of some austerity type freight locomotives and a relatively small number of tank engines it had been a 'make do and mend' environment on our railways. There were huge arrears of maintenance and severe prioritisation had been necessary for many years. It would only be a government cheque book that in the long run could restore our railways to pre-war standards. As a result a decision was made to Nationalise Britain's railways.

Lost in the mist of time is the sheer size of the nationalised undertaking. Shortly after the creation of what affectionately became known as 'BR' the manpower employed by British Railways was a staggering 635,000. At the beginning of 1949 BR operated over 20,000 locomotives (many of them Victorian), 55,000 passenger vehicles and over 1,100,000 freight wagons. These wagons had an average capacity of 14.5 tons (about one-fifth of the capacity of a modern bogie wagon). For completeness of statistics there were over 52,000 railway-operated road vehicles and 132 ships. There were 19,631 railway route miles and 52,235 miles of standard gauge track on the BR network.

From 1 January 1948, British Railways came under the Railway Executive umbrella, which in turn was responsible through the British Transport Commission to the government and therefore the British public. The idea was for a method known as 'functional' management to be employed, which theoretically ensured a standardisation of practice and coordination of action throughout British Railways 'with all their (existing) inherited individual divergent practices'. With some wonderful senior management gobbledegook the objective was for new standards to 'become effective as quickly as possible thus facilitating the uniformity of management from which simplicity of working and economy of administration can most readily be achieved'! As if reading from a training session 'white board', the policy for the proper use of the various forms of transport, which could not fail to benefit the country's economic position, besides yielding a more efficient service to the traveller and trader, was to assemble all information, analyse that information and develop the future based on the results of that analysis. Theoretically, this was all fine-sounding as it was no doubt drafted by a 'Sir Humphrey' type of civil servant.

The Railway Executive went to some lengths to explain that contrary to popular belief the creation of British Railways and its division into regions was not simply the perpetuation of the 'Big Four', particularly as there were six regions. Although here we are concerned with goods and freight trains it is worthwhile recording the geographical divisions behind the formulation of the regions. The Western and Southern Regions contained in general terms the same respective systems as those formerly belonging to the Great Western and Southern Railways. Scotland became a separate region in its own right.

The London Midland Region comprised the English and North Wales lines of the former London Midland & Scottish Railway, plus the former joint Cheshire lines, but with the Central and South Wales lines being transferred to the Western Region, and the London, Tilbury & Southend lines to the Eastern Region. The Eastern Region comprised that part of the erstwhile London & North Eastern Railway which extended from Leeds and Doncaster to London, with all the East Anglian and Lincolnshire lines. The North Eastern Region was roughly the same as the old pre-Grouping North Eastern Railway, stretching north of Doncaster and Leeds to Berwick, embracing the principal lines bounded by the Tweed, the Humber and the Pennines. There were a number of minor exceptions.

Whatever the composition of the structure of the new organisation, one of the evergreen problems concerned finance. Under the 1947 Transport Act the British Transport

Commission was required to prepare a scheme, or schemes, of charges covering the various services and facilities for which it was responsible. One of the first criticisms of the railways was directed at their fares and freight rates. By 1948 they were 55 per cent above the rates prevailing in 1939. In a problem that still exists today, the BTC was well aware that between 1939 and 1948 the price of major commodities and materials used by the railway had escalated beyond reason, including iron and steel, a 100 per cent increase, rubber 130 per cent, non-ferrous metals 136 per cent, coal 174 per cent, lubricating oils 114 per cent, canvas 237 per cent, paint 229 per cent, uniforms 300 per cent, and timbers for sleepers 344 per cent. Top of the list was linseed oil at 450 per cent.

Although wages were not high, certainly by modern standards and in real terms, in 1939 the 560,000 staff of the 'Big Four' earned £105 million (about £3.60 per week average) whereas after the end of hostilities, 597,000 staff were earning £182 million. By the end of 1948 the 635,000 staff were earning a whopping £233 million (just over £7 per week average)! Unification of the railways did produce some manpower savings and between 10 July 1948 and 26 March 1949 railway manpower reduced by 27,800, much of it by natural wastage. A few other interesting statistics show that in 1948 there was a staggering figure of fewer than 1 billion passenger journeys originating on all regions of British Railways and total passenger miles exceeded 21 billion. A total of 750 special trains were run carrying over 3 million passengers, an average of 400 per special train.

Here we are specifically concerned with goods and freight trains and there were some interesting facts and figures relating to such services. In 1948 over 276 million tons of freight and merchandise were carried on BR, but the most amazing statistic was that of this total 160 million tons was in the 'coal' class of traffic, about 58 per cent of the entire rail-borne goods volumes! The Railway Executive announced in their 1949 review that, following an extensive study of industrial need and existing schedules, 316 new daily freight services had been introduced during the first year of Nationalisation while 495 other freight services had been accelerated. Intermediate delays had been reduced, parallel services where possible had been combined, and the number of express freight trains travelling at speeds approaching those of passenger schedules had been considerably increased. By the end of 1948 these trains were covering 61,000 miles weekly, while semi-express freight train mileage came to 240,000 miles per week.

With the exception of a little short-distance traffic and a 'few million' tons moved by canal, every ton of coal conveyed by rail in the entire UK travelled on average a distance of

▼ The outside-cylinder Billinton K class 2-6-0 Moguls dated back to 1913 and comprised a popular class of just 17 locomotives that were mainly used on London Brighton & South Coast Railway lines. Proudly showing its new British Railways livery and number, No 32344 passes Durrington-on-Sea in August 1949 with a Portsmouth to Brighton goods train. A Lancing-built brake van can be seen immediately behind the tender. The background fields were soon to be completely covered by a housing estate, while top left is Highdown Hill, part of the South Downs. *R.A.H. Baxter*

55 miles. This movement of coal to gas works, electricity power stations, coke ovens, iron and steel works, and industry generally, as well as for domestic use was provided by a stock of over half a million coal wagons, which in 1948, despite having various names painted on their sides, were all owned by the BTC. It is now hard to imagine 500,000 wagons full of anything! The distribution of empty wagons, according to the varying needs of the different Divisions of the National Coal Board (the coal industry had also been Nationalised) and individual pits was equitably arranged by specialised wagon control centres working by telephone and a mass of numerical data, relating to the demand of every single rail-connected coal mine in the country. The Railway Executive pointed out that the movement of loaded coal wagons was no haphazard business and involved detailed planning and, wherever possible, block trains would be made up. Eventually, the words 'block train' would describe the only significantly viable freight loads on the BR network.

In the light of goods and freight by rail developments in the 21st century, some of the terminology used in 1949 by the Railway Executive is quite amusing, such as 'household removals can be conveniently undertaken by railways who give an all-in service and offer to members of the household a reduction in the passenger fares to the new home town station'. Also 'the facilities covered the requirements of ordinary householders or the complete removal of a farmer, comprising his own effects, equipment and livestock by special train, if necessary with the tending of cattle and other stock en route.'

Special arrangements could be made for the complete removal of companies involving both their staff and equipment. Under the heading of 'Container Transport' the Executive was way ahead of its time by confirming that the container method of transport had the advantage of door-to-door conveyance thereby saving in packing costs and speeding up delivery. There were general containers but special units were available for such things as furniture, cycles, bricks and tiles, while for meat and similar perishables ventilated and insulated containers were provided, although publicity stopped short of offering refrigerated containers.

At this time BR was modernising its collection and delivery arrangements, as fast as new vehicles could be obtained. Highlighted were the new type of 'mechanical horse' and the experiments being conducted with 'electric' horse tractors. There were 12,500 motors in the BR collection and delivery fleet, but a startling admission was that in 1948 over 7,000 horses were still used by the railway in a wide range of capacities! There was an amazing array of vehicles in the fleet ranging from small parcels vans to high-capacity goods tractors and trailers, effectively articulated lorries. Also included were some rather fine internal combustion-engined horse-boxes and vehicles for other livestock as well as the romantically described 'country lorry'.

One of the great disadvantages of conveying goods and freight by rail has always been the difficulty in providing satisfactory 'door-to-door' arrangements. If a company has to purchase commercial vehicles to transport goods

▼ Over 100 miles north of the location featured in the last photograph, but taken just one month later, on 10 September 1949, is this view at Handsworth Junction featuring the Stetchford goods train. Interestingly, the 'British Railways' stencil has been applied to the tender of this Stanier 2-6-0, but the locomotive shows the early BR number M2951 (later No 42951). Again, there is a wonderfully mixed load behind the locomotive. *W.A. Camwell/SLS*

and materials from a railway goods yard or freight terminal to, say, a factory, then they might as well utilise the same vehicle to convey the item from that factory to customer. The railways realised the problem and the executive were trying to rapidly expand a network that covered the entire country with zonal collection and delivery services, which would provide for the concentration of what they called 'smalls' traffic at railheads and to use road services complementary to rail in the process of providing door-to-door delivery. An integrated transport service was an essential ingredient of the 1947 Transport Act and BR and the Executive were trying their best within many constraints to provide such a service. They also encouraged the laying of private goods sidings and promised an advisory service for new works and the layout of sidings.

One of the most important aspects was motive power where, years before the 'BR Standard' classes of locomotive appeared, it had been recognised 'there should be as few classes (of steam locomotive) as possible, one suited to each of several sorts of traffic, citing express passenger, ordinary passenger, heavy goods, shunting, and so forth', while recognising that the ideal would be about a dozen classes of standard locomotive types. It was admitted that this was a tall order for an organisation that had inherited widely varying equipment from four different companies, which in their turn still possessed, at the end of their existence, hundreds of locomotives that had been inherited from their pre-Grouping predecessors. The situation presented BR with a formidable opportunity to scrap and build, reducing no fewer than 400 classes of locomotive to just 12. The Executive did not favour taking the best of what already existed, which they said would lead to stagnation. They were keen for any standardisation to be kept fluid and open to new ideas and improvements. They intended to build prototypes of advanced designs and by continuous experiment try out improvements and modifications. These would be re-examined and tested leading to a 'Mark II' version of what had been called standard.

Of the 'Big Four' companies the Railway Executive singled out the London Midland & Scottish Railway as an example of what could be achieved in terms of standardisation, even though far removed from the envisaged plan. In 1923, the LMSR had inherited 10,316 locomotives of 400 different classes, but by the end of 1945 they had reduced the total to 8,089 in 'only' 133 classes. However, before the 'standard' classes could be produced it was decided to conduct 'Locomotive Exchanges' whereby locomotives could be tested on different regions in different environments with a view to ascertaining the best that the former railway companies had produced. Much has been written about these exchanges and although certain characteristics were identified, overall they were inconclusive in terms of the optimum locomotive. It was not only performance and traction that was tested but also, for example, coal consumption.

In 1948, 410 locomotives were built and 769 were pensioned off. As at 1 January 1949 there were 20,216 steam locomotives in service on British Railways compared with 20,030 a year earlier, while in 1949 it was intended to build 465 new locomotives with 758 heavy freight War Department engines previously on loan to be taken into BR stock. These were the 2-8-0 and 2-10-0 WD class of locomotive. The forecast date for the first 'standard' class of steam locomotive to hit the rails was 1951. Surprisingly, diesel and gas turbine traction was given short shrift by the Railway Executive on the grounds that 'ours is a great coal-producing country and the birthplace of the steam locomotive, Britain is traditionally regarded as "steam' country".

It was recognised that BR had 904 route miles and 2,094 track miles of electrically operated lines, but in terms of details the following was their short comment. 'For some railway purposes the internal combustion engine offers the alternative advantages of instant readiness and a greater continuity of availability, although the initial costs of such units are higher than those of steam locomotives. Diesel and electric locomotives are particularly suitable for continuous shunting duties and 65 such units are owned by BR. A total of 28 350hp shunters are on order and one 800hp example. Tests have been made with 1,600hp and 3,200hp diesels in main line service, the aristocrats of this form of traction, and another type of main line diesel is on order. An experimental gas turbine locomotive is shortly to be tested in service.'

The unification of the railways had thrown up a surplus of open wagons. Some 85,000 obsolete examples were being scrapped under a three-year programme, saving £5 million in maintenance. BR still owned 1,165,000 wagons, an almost unbelievable number today. In 1949 it was envisaged that 27,225 new freight wagons would be built, including 13,248 mineral wagons, 4,354 ordinary open wagons, and 4,166 covered wagons. If it had not been for a shortage of raw materials and workshop capacity BR would have procured 35–40,000 new goods and freight vehicles.

BR had inherited a complete rag-bag of goods wagons. Technologically little had changed for decades and although wagons with dumb buffers and no brakes were confined to self-contained industrial sites, there were thousands upon thousands of wagons with no continuous brake, where train guards had to manually pin down and pick up the brakes on many steeply graded routes. Even what are now deemed to be old 'vacuum-braked' wagons were, proportionally, and as expressed as a percentage of the whole fleet, thin on the ground. In 1948, air brakes on goods wagons were unheard of and the wheelbase of the majority of wagons was short, which added to instability at anything above moderate speeds. Payloads were extremely modest and there was a plethora of three, five and seven-plank wooden-bodied wagons throughout the network. A tare of 8 to 15 tons per wagon was commonplace and wagons such as the small vacuum-braked OOVs were still

▲ With such a vast number of steam locomotives in stock, repainting of the entire BR fleet could not take place overnight and, indeed, some hints of pre-Nationalisation ownership continued into the 1950s. On 16 April 1949, 1898-built C12 class 4-4-2T No 7385, soon to be 67385, is seen at Saffron Walden with the daily goods for Bartlow, as the signalman poses beside his box with the single-line token. The last such freight ran in December 1964, passenger trains having ceased in September 1964; a classic Beeching-era closure. *W.A. Camwell/SLS*

▼ In this further remarkable post-Nationalisation photograph from 1949, the expression 'weed-covered track' would seem to be almost an understatement. Finding a path through the undergrowth at the disused station of Tongwynlais on the Rhydyfelin branch on 16 September is former Rhymney Railway 0-6-2T No 66, with perhaps half a dozen wagons for Nantgarw Colliery. The end is obviously nigh. *SLS*

being built as late as 1960, and were in use in Cornwall for conveying china clay until 1988. Bogie wagons existed only for special loads.

The other major problem experienced by the Railway Executive was concerned with the lack of modern mechanisation for loading and unloading wagons. In many cases, where such equipment existed, mechanisation was confined to primitive short conveyor belts and small-capacity cranes. To some extent this was outside the control of the railways, but there was little point in developing and supplying newer high-capacity wagons of a modern design if a lack of investment at the pit head or foundry relied on age-old practices and ancient wagon-loading equipment. Even today there is an element of 'grab discharge' unloading, which takes considerably longer than an on-the-move hopper discharge system. Over the years many goods yards had the fundamentals of loading docks and site cranes available, but positioning wagons was an extremely time-consuming business. Typical BR wagon turn-round times were a very pedestrian 11.9 days, as mentioned earlier, although in most cases the customer was complicit in these delays.

Another major headache for the newly nationalised railways was the coordination of traffic flows. Nearly every station of any size had its own dedicated goods yard and as the so-called Beeching report would later emphasise this method of handling goods was hopelessly uneconomic with no prospect whatsoever of producing a positive commercial return. Not only was the size of the goods and freight network a problem but many of our larger marshalling yards and concentration freight depots had not been modernised. Other than for the few standard block loads, shunting movements could be lengthy and complex as individual wagonloads were coupled into their next formation to reach sometimes distant destinations, or be correctly positioned for the next local trip working. With old operating methods and a slow paper-driven administration system it is no wonder that the road lobby were rubbing their hands with glee as post-war commerce gradually changed into top gear.

The Railway Executive also had comprehensive plans for railway works, signalling, telecommunications, marshalling yards, track, stations and motive power depots, but alas, as we will see in the next chapter, making the railway pay was mission impossible. The consumption of materials by railways was enormous, including over 15 million tons of coal per annum, 600,000 tons of steel and 436,000 tons of timber. What was needed in a steam-driven labour-intensive age was a robust and fully funded modernisation plan. The Modernisation Plan was to emerge in the 1950s, but the entire subject of funding was a political football that demanded deep government pockets full of taxpayer's money, a massively reduced workforce, and a considerable amount of courage!

▼ The entire Immingham area continues to be extremely busy for freight traffic, the main payloads presently being iron ore, imported coal and petrochemical products. However, it is now many years since passenger trains served the dock area, the surviving passenger routes being between Barnetby, Grimsby and Cleethorpes plus the branch line to Barton-on-Humber. Immingham Dock station once enjoyed two routes, to Goxhill and Ulceby, but they closed in 1963 and 1969 respectively. In the early days of Nationalisation A5 class 4-6-2T No 69820 heads a train at Immingham Dock station that demonstrates what a run-down state BR was in, judging by the motley collection of coaches any passengers had to choose from. The small box van in this interesting consist looks somewhat incongruous. *SLS*

▲ Many of the country junction stations had the most wonderful running-in boards and that at Bartlow on the borders of Essex and Cambridgeshire was no exception. There will be no passengers to read the sign proclaiming 'Bartlow change for Ashdon Halt & Saffron Walden' on this train, a Cambridge to Marks Tey goods on 16 April 1949. Heading the ramshackle consist is Holden J17 class 0-6-0 No 65575, which looks very uncared for. The engine carries its new BR number but not yet on a smokebox plate, being painted on the bufferbeam while the tender still shows 'LNER'. *W.A. Camwell/SLS*

▼ One can almost hear the banking engines 'shouting' as the little and large combination of 'Jinty' 0-6-0T No 47565 and the mighty 'Big Bertha' 0-10-0 No 58100, built by the Midland Railway in 1919 to a Fowler design specifically for such duties, make for an unusual-looking pairing. The train is pounding through Bromsgrove station and is so long that the 1-in-37 incline beyond the road bridge can be clearly distinguished. The northbound goods was photographed on 30 April 1949. *W.A. Camwell/SLS*

▲ Looking considerably older than its 1920 build date Pickersgill-designed Caledonian Railway 3P 4-4-0 No 14507, in fact a not-yet renumbered BR No 54507 and still in its pre-Nationalisation LMS garb, passes Auchengray in Lanarkshire, between Carstairs and Edinburgh, with a pick-up goods on 9 June 1949. At the time of Nationalisation BR operated over 20,000 steam locomotives, many of them ancient, and well over one million goods wagons. The fireman seems to be dangling his leg out of the cab!
W.A. Camwell/SLS

▼ In typical post-Second World War condition, but with its number and 'LMS' identifier having been wiped clean on depot by an oily rag in the then recent past, 0-4-4T No 1338 was just four months away from Nationalisation when photographed passing Bengeworth with an Evesham (Midland) to Ashchurch goods on 26 August 1947. The train crew were no doubt surprised that such a mundane working was being photographed and it has sadly taken over 65 years for their footplate portraits to appear in print. At the time they were part of a vast national railway workforce of 635,000, which BR was to inherit. *SLS*

DEMISE OF THE GOODS YARD

▲ This 1914 view of the old Midland & Great Northern Junction Railway terminus of Norwich City station is of particular interest in that it shows just how important goods traffic was in those far-off days. There are miscellaneous box vans and open wagons, produce baskets and porters' trolleys as well as some distant passenger stock. Road transport would soon be making its mark as the motor lorry developed and became cheaper, faster and more reliable than the railways. *LGRP/SLS*

▼ Most stations as distinct from halts had some form of goods-handling track work, whether it was a single siding, a loading dock or a functional goods yard. At most sites loading and unloading was a manual process, although some yards had low-capacity cranes. This coal, seen on the goods platform at Claverdon, between Hatton and Stratford-upon-Avon, is being bagged straight from the coal wagons in hundredweight sacks for local distribution. *LGRP/SLS*

▲ Rowsley, north-west of Matlock on the old Midland Railway route, has an interesting history. The original terminus of the line from Ambergate was opened in 1849 but when the through route across the Peak District opened in 1862 the terminus was closed to passengers. From 1862 to 1968 the site was retained but for goods only, a most unusual situation for such a lengthy period. In this charming view the old station, goods shed and cattle pens are all visible as well as an interesting assortment of four-wheeled wagons. One wonders whether the tapered lamp heads in the left foreground were simply scrapped after closure. *W.A. Camwell/SLS*

▼ Long before the age of modern metal containers was born BR operated their own container service under the 'Door to Door' marketing name. The effort needed to provide the service was considerable because BR had to supply road transport at both ends of the journey, a costly business both in terms of capital outlay and manpower. In the background are a large number of National Carriers trailers while in the foreground we are treated to a wonderful display of wagons, some vacuum-brake fitted, some not. The scene is the former Southern Railway goods depot at Plymouth Friary, on 21 September 1974. *R.F. Roberts/SLS*

▲ Dieselisation has arrived in Cornwall as this scene at Truro Yard is shared between 5700 class 0-6-0PT No 3702 and English Electric shunter No D3510, later Class 08 No 08395. The photograph was taken on 15 October 1958, just five months after the diesel locomotive was built. The steam-hauled local freight is on the up main line and in the left background is the motive power depot and to the right the repair shops. There is now no freight traffic whatsoever at Truro, except for a weekly tanker train that simply passes by. *B.A. Butt*

▼ The goods trains in the post-Nationalisation era were utterly fascinating in that the permutation of wagon types was seemingly infinite. In this view there are cattle wagons, containers, five- and seven-plank open wagons, a hopper wagon, two withdrawn passenger coaches, box vans and more than one brake van. Class 4F 0-6-0 No 44579 of Hellifield shed is working hard with an up goods as it passes Calverley & Rodley station between Shipley and Leeds, on 27 February 1960. Today there are just two electrified lines at this location, which is devoid of two of the four main lines and all the sidings visible here. The coaches in the sidings here were used only on bank holidays; how times change! *Gavin Morrison*

► This elevated view shows the staggering railway infrastructure to the north-east of Wakefield Kirkgate, in the vicinity of Turners Lane Junction on the old Lancashire & Yorkshire Railway route. Goodness knows where all of these assorted wagons were destined, or how long it would be before they continued their journeys. What is perhaps surprising in view of traffic volumes is that the photograph was taken by the author as recently as May 1966. Demoted to humble freight duty is 'Jubilee' 4-6-0 No 45694 *Bellerophon* working from Healey Mills towards Normanton. This 'goods' scene has gone forever and is much lamented by many. *Author*

▼ When the BR Modernisation Plan was drawn up in the early 1950s a significant investment was made in large 'hump' marshalling yards where state-of-the-art, but now primitive, technology was incorporated in the wagon movement business. Wagons would be propelled to the top of a small hill or 'hump' and then released to roll down through a series of points to one of many sidings, where other wagons for the next common hub or destination would be located.

Retarders were used to control the speed of wagons to ensure that any meeting of buffers was as gentle as possible. Few such yards were fully utilised. Built specially for such yards were the Class 13 hump shunters, formed as master and slave units. No 13001 is seen at Sheffield's Tinsley Yard in November 1979. Unbelievably, the yard would fall into disuse within a decade. *Author*

▲ Having featured very full and partially full goods yards we now see the next stage of BR freight deterioration where acres and acres of sidings gradually became disused as the hopelessly uneconomic wagonload freight and then 'Speedlink' services were withdrawn. This dismal scene shows the once-important location of Severn Tunnel Junction in April 1984. Passing the silent sidings is a Railfreight-liveried Class 47 with some MoD munition wagons from Glascoed. In earlier years there would be a long line of up to a dozen diesel locomotives in the sidings above the train. *Author*

▼ Other than for sites being totally razed this must be the final ignominy in the life cycle of a large marshalling yard. Viewing scores of completely abandoned sidings this was the sad scene from the control tower of Whitemoor Yard at March in Cambridgeshire during August 1985. A few years earlier the yard would have been bursting with wagons conveying every conceivable commodity, but particularly agricultural produce from the Fens. For those who worked in the yard a way of life had truly ended. *Author*

▲ As the goods, freight and marshalling yards closed BR entered the real estate business as the BR Property Board made a fortune by selling off abandoned buildings and large tracts of land. Many fine buildings, once the pride and joy of the pre-Grouping railway companies, fell into a state of decay and were subsequently demolished. This edifice was once Canon's Marsh goods depot in Bristol, seen here on 28 April 1979. The adjacent goods line from Ashton Bridge Junction closed in June 1965. *R.F. Roberts/SLS*

▼ In some of our major cities the amount of land owned by BR was phenomenal, and much of it was prime land not far from city centres. This vast warehouse and adjacent sidings was the Great Northern Railway's main goods warehouse in Manchester and it was located relatively near to Central station. Photographed on 16 October 1976, it now seems inconceivable that such a magnificent industrial building could fall into disuse, but the same could be said about hundreds upon hundreds of textile mills in both Lancashire and Yorkshire. *R.F. Roberts/SLS*

MODERNISATION AND BEECHING

THERE WAS NO DOUBT THAT DESPITE the gradual arrival of new equipment, progress in the rolling stock and locomotive departments was painfully slow and an all-embracing forward-looking modernisation plan was required. Whatever proposals emerged it was clear that it would only be the HM Treasury that could afford radical change. In the early 1950s the railways actually made a small operating profit, but this was against a somewhat artificial situation where there was only modest capital investment due to the post-war catch-up process on long overdue maintenance tasks. Adding to the potential difficulties for the railways was a resurgent road transport industry where the problems of wartime and rationing were becoming distant memories. The Modernisation Plan was published in December 1954, but typical of the way that Westminster works there had to be agreement on the way forward not only from all internal departments within the railway industry but the huge package had to have HM Treasury approval or at least agreement in principle to the proposals.

The plan involved wide-ranging change including the electrification of principal routes, large-scale dieselisation and the eventual abandonment of the steam locomotive, new passenger rolling stock and freight wagons, resignalling and track renewal with an objective of speeding up most services (at least 100mph on main lines), and the closure of duplicate and heavy loss-making lines. (See the companion volumes *The Rise and Fall of British Railways: Main Line Diesel Locomotives* and *The Rise and Fall of British Railways: Branch and Minor Lines* for more details about non-freight issues.) In total at 1955 values the financial bottom line on expenditure for the Modernisation Plan was a staggering £1.2 billion, over £22 billion at today's values, although this huge expenditure was to be staged over a decade and a half, with an element of self-financing.

Other than for the upgrading of the permanent way and signalling the main advantage as far as goods and freight traffic were concerned was the £125 million to be invested in 2,500 diesel locomotives. Also specific in goods and freight terms was the whopping £140 million that was designated for improvements of goods yards, and a significant £225 million for investment in freight wagons. Changes were going to be dramatic with 150 major freight yards being replaced by 55 new or reconstructed central yards, which would incorporate advanced technology including mechanisation, many on the 'hump' shunting principle.

There would be considerable rationalisation on the freight scene as trip working was to be greatly reduced by closing old small yards and focussing the traffic on larger concentration yards. BR wanted to eliminate the time-consuming process of pinning down and picking up brakes on goods trains and they proposed to fit all goods wagons with continuous vacuum brakes, a truly gargantuan task. This process would save 10,000 hours per week, eliminate thousands of catch points and generally speed up the entire freight business and increase line capacity. Although new four-wheeled wagons were ordered the railways were frustrated in that the loading and track infrastructure, for example at collieries, could not cope with wagons over 24.5 tons in gross weight, whereas BR wanted to order high-capacity bogie wagons. One new target set was to reduce wagon turn-round time by 30 per cent and if achieved the wagon fleet could be reduced from 1,141,500 to 752,000, a reduction of nearly 400,000 wagons. It was also the intention to eliminate old grease-lubricated bearings, which needed constant maintenance if hot running and bearing failure were to be avoided.

With the closure of so many lines throughout the 1950s, long before Dr Richard (later Lord) Beeching arrived on the scene, there was an impact on total freight tonnage carried by the railways. However, many analysts would point out that tonnage in itself was not the criterion, but profitable tonnage was!

The Modernisation Plan was approved and to some considerable degree implemented, but in retrospect many regarded the exercise as an opportunity missed. Judgements were undoubtedly influenced by the continuing losses on British Railways, while the railway continued to do battle against music hall jokes aimed at the heart of the industry with, curiously, curled-up BR buffet sandwiches featuring with monotonous regularity. In modern 'speak' the railways could have done with some public relations spin doctor or evangelist from the deep south to get their message across. In fact, it was not until the early 1980s and the arrival of DJ Jimmy Savile that BR used advertising as a 'PR' exercise. He was associated with railway publicity for some time with his long-running 'This is the age of the train' series of adverts. Sadly, BR was continuing to be a serious drain on the public purse and just as the Modernisation Plan was intended to promote the railways something equally radical had to be done to slow or halt the continuing financial deficit in a nation that was becoming increasingly car conscious.

The growth in certain types of rail traffic did not happen and in goods and freight terms the vast number of tracks in new yards and the general scale of operations envisaged never materialised. Many classes of diesel freight locomotives were planned for light freight use and yet the era of the lightweight, branch line and trip freight workings was coming to an end. There was simply no work for these locomotives to do, which in many cases was just as well because there were so many unreliable and untested 'bad buys' around the network that chaos may have ensued. For example, Classes 15, 16, 17, 21, 22 and 23 were all operational disasters and millions upon millions of pounds of public money was squandered in a very short space of time. In some cases repeat orders for locomotives that had not turned a wheel were made. The Class 17 'Claytons' were eight times less reliable than the English Electric Class 20s. Withdrawals of the 'Claytons' started in 1968, just three years after the last-built example was delivered. Introduced in 1962, by 1971 the entire fleet of 117 locomotives had been withdrawn from service on BR. There were many planning disasters, but one of the most scandalous events was ordering no fewer than 1,200 diesel shunter units at a time when shunting requirements were rapidly diminishing.

The Modernisation Plan had brought about change but there were also many failures. For example, in the aforementioned goods and freight arena the huge investment made in marshalling yards and concentration goods depots completely ignored the serious contraction in wagonload freight traffic. In short and in wagon movement percentage terms, there was little that required marshalling! However, one of the long-time strangleholds imposed on our railways was the scale of charges that it could levy upon its customers.

In 1957, the Transport Tribunal confirmed a Railway Merchandise Charges Scheme, which set maximum charges operative from 1 July, leaving the railway with 'relative' freedom to fix charges within such maxima. Through the requirements of the 1947 and 1953 Transport Acts the government had regard to BR charging customers either maximum charges or 'reasonable' charges. Maximum charges were graduated according to consignment weight and loadability, with distinctions being made between bulk traffic and general traffic. Charges for carriage and associated services were also taken into consideration. The situation was hugely complicated, caused by the vast number of charges applicable, which were predicated not only by weight, category (including dangerous goods) and claims risk, but spread across three levels: between principal stations, between a principal and a minor station, and between minor stations. This scheme was intended to improve and update the charges applicable for the goods and freight by rail business, but a BR brochure of the era almost boasted that 'the retention of nearly a *million* rates in this way will provide for the vast majority of wagon load consignments now going by rail'.

These charges may have been fair in terms of public acceptability, but they needed to be simpler and more business-like and to have a direct link to the overall costs including overheads, such as depreciation on fixed assets employed in actually conveying the commodity by rail. From the taxpayer's perspective if it was cheaper to ship certain goods by road then they should not have been conveyed by train at a loss. To retain such an unbelievably

▼ Back in March 1953 most private cars on the roads were of British manufacture and were black. Adding just a touch of colour is this BR van, No A631W, registration HYR 544. BR owned a huge lorry and van fleet for a multitude of purposes, ranging from goods and freight deliveries to the movement of minor parcels traffic, as well as internal stores movements. With BR totem transfers applied this vehicle is standing in front of the old Plymouth North Road station.
British Railways (Western Region)

complex system by the BTC was hard to comprehend. The entire goods and freight management structure across BR was also incredibly complex. Just on the Western Region there were four District Goods Managers and eight District Commercial Managers! It is little wonder the entire national operation was regarded as cumbersome.

Promised savings were never delivered and the BR deficit was £68 million in 1960, £87 million in 1961 and £102 million in 1962 (£2 billion in 2012 values). This pattern was repeated in other large nationalised industries, particularly coal, and it was clear to all but the illiterate that large monolithic nationalised industries were grossly inefficient, were difficult to dissect into specific businesses, or to expose them to competition. In fact, in 1960 the National Coal Board lost £64 million, just a shade less than the railways. This position was unsustainable, especially to a car owner with oil-fired heating whose income tax was already too high! Accordingly it was the Conservative government headed by Harold McMillan that passed the 1962 Transport Act, which abolished the BTC and created the British Railways Board (BRB). The Minister of Transport appointed industrialist Dr Richard Beeching as Chairman hoping that good business ideas from the private sector might change the course of the loss-making BR super tanker that was seemingly impossible to stop.

Beeching's approach was to examine closely the viability of the railways from what, in outside corporate terms, would have been business sectors. Beeching demonstrated that there had been a degree of mismanagement because he found that not all of the relevant statistics required for him and his team to conduct the review were available, and valuable time was lost conducting surveys and embarking on fact-finding exercises. Beeching's findings were pretty grim and it was obvious that hard choices would need to be made if deficits were to be reduced and to this extent he intended to provide a number of options for the politicians to consider.

At the end of the day, Beeching knew that there was not a hope of the railways paying their way and the objective became one of minimising losses by eliminating the most financially hopeless areas of operation. However, the report made it clear that where it was identified that the development of a service in a particular way could make them more efficient and satisfactory than alternative forms of transport, improvements would be recommended.

Some aspects of Beeching's work must have been depressing in that while economies were being made throughout BR during 1962, two pay increases amounting to just over 9 per cent were awarded to BR employees and the working week was reduced, just the medicine required for a loss-making business! The answer to ever-rising payroll costs was to reduce manpower and this was achieved. In 1953, 594,000 staff were employed on the railways but by 1973 this had been reduced to 223,000 and, by comparison, by 1993 it was 115,000. The fact was that in

1961 with the sole exception of coal traffic, which made a tiny profit, none of the main classes of goods and freight traffic covered their full costs. There was a huge disparity between classes of traffic. Wagonload general merchandise, which loaded badly and gave rise to very little through train movement, was a serious loss maker.

Sundries traffic was a financial liability for the same reason. The two types of freight traffic that showed the best margin over direct costs were minerals and coal. Of these coal gave a small margin of profit over full cost, while mineral traffic fell just short of doing so. These two classes gave a much higher proportion of through train movement with well-loaded trains. However, the long-term future of British coal gave little room for confidence.

In 1961, of the 17,800 route miles of track on the BR network 4,100 were open for freight only. Excluding parcels and mails the total receipts for freight traffic were £255.6 million and direct costs were £268.5 million, an annual loss of £12.9 million, but when allocated indirect costs were added (and it was fair to distribute a whole range of overheads across the various heads of income) this rose to a net revenue deficit of £76 million. Some scary statistics emerged; for example, one-third of the total BR track mileage carried only 1 per cent of freight traffic. Similarly, half of the total BR route mileage carried only 5 per cent of total freight ton miles. The conclusion was that over half of the BR system earned far less than was sufficient to cover the cost of providing a passenger or freight service.

The report pointed out that to make matters worse the type of traffic on these loss-making lines was of a less favourable kind, and that their contribution in terms of marginal revenue was small, if not negative. As regards freight stations, one-third of them produced less than 1 per cent of the station freight receipts and one-half of the stations produced less than 3 per cent. In other words, 50 per cent of freight stations could be closed completely with gross receipts falling only from 100 to 97 per cent of the then current levels.

One of the most damning statements in the report that was hard to refute was as follows. 'It will be seen that the gross revenue derived from traffic of all kinds flowing from the least used half of the total number of British Railways' stations does not match the cost of the stations themselves. In other words it makes no contribution whatever to route costs, to movement costs, nor to terminal costs at the other end of its transits. There can be no question, therefore, that the railways would be better off financially if a high proportion of the stations were closed, even if this resulted in a total loss of the traffic passing through them.'

At this time the age of the motor car and the heavy lorry was upon the nation and to cater for the anticipated growth a network of motorways was being built. Again, the UK was arriving late in the day as in other countries the extensive use of autobahns, autostrade, freeways etc. was already well established. These much-needed (and now grossly inadequate) motorways gave a boost to road hauliers, especially in what had hitherto and in railway terminology been smaller consignments carried by wagonload freight. In many cases the new-generation lorries carried a heavier payload than certain railway wagons, while offering a door-to-door service and without the risk of supplies and goods being interrupted by failures or strikes.

Again the freight statistics were appalling, even allowing for margins of variation. For example, in 1961 145.7 million tons of coal were moved from the 600 rail-connected collieries, making BR a paltry £2.8 million profit over total costs. Mineral traffic totalled 54.3 million tons with a loss against full costs of £3.7 million. However, general merchandise including wagonload freight and sundries totalled 38.2 million tons with losses of £75.1 million! The general merchandise position was indefensible and even superman could not have turned that business around.

The massive dilemma for BR was that the total ton mileage of coal was seen as more likely to decrease than increase (it had decreased by some 29 million tons between 1953 and 1961) and even if it did increase, any gains would be very marginal because the railways already carried the majority of coal. Furthermore, out of the 145.7 tons moved by rail only 27.6m tons were for domestic use and this was rapidly decreasing. The same situation prevailed for minerals whereby the railways carried a very high proportion of the total traffic of that kind and any increase was likely to be small. The only opportunity for significant growth in tonnage carried was in general merchandise, but whether further modernisation and improvements in general handling would win market share, not to mention become profitable, was an unknown quantity, but unlikely.

Coal traffic could have been far more profitable but there were many factors that worked against the railways. The first problem was the multiplicity of destinations for the coal. Although 57 million tons was moved by through train operation, effectively block loads, 89 million tons was moved by the staging of wagons, with 54 million tons going to private sidings and 35 million tons to stations. At 14.5 tons of coal per wagon it cost nearly twice as much per ton to deliver single wagon consignments to such locations compared with a wagon included in a block load (95p versus 53p per ton). There were variations in the quality and type of coal, which complicated the distribution process.

None of the 600 rail-served collieries had meaningful storage bunkers or facilities for the rapid loading of trains and, instead, railway wagons were effectively used as storage bunkers, which required a vast number of wagons for the purpose. These wagons stood at the collieries for an average of two days and the National Coal Board paid nothing for the privilege of using BR assets in this way! The NCB used BR wagons for their own purpose for about 22 million wagon days per annum at an estimated cost to the railways of £11 million, whereas the NCB paid BR a mere £1 million for demurrage. These wagon delays also occurred at the receiving end of the journey, ports being singled out as the worst offenders.

▼ A railway modeller's delight is this almost toy train comprising an 1883 Drummond 'standard goods' 0-6-0 in the 3F power category heading just two wagons, one containing a generator, and a 'Shark' style of brake van. It is hardly surprising that there is steam to spare as veteran No 57274 trundles past Prestwick, just north of Ayr during 1959. Note the old bullhead jointed rail, a rapidly disappearing feature on today's railways. *Gavin Morrison*

Showing good business acumen and remarkable foresight, especially in terms of what evolved in later years with the 'merry-go-round' operation, Beeching commented: 'The degree to which the position is unsatisfactory is made more apparent when consideration is given to the supply [of coal] to new power stations. To take advantage of new locomotives and make rail haul more efficient, the sound course is to use large, braked, hopper wagons, which have a better load/tare weight ratio, which can be drawn at high speed, and which can be unloaded very quickly at the receiving terminal. Such wagons are relatively costly, but are much more economical to use if they can be turned around quickly. They are, however, too expensive to be used as storage bunkers at the pits, and need to be loaded quickly from static bunkers.' As aforementioned, the major problem was the lack of rapid loading facilities at the pits, many of which dated back to Victorian times.

Although many pundits complained about Beeching and challenged some of the figures that he and his team came up with, the statistics were so bad that even if such figures had been 100 per cent out, which they were not, the goods and freight picture would still have been dire. For example, in 1960 there were 5,031 stations open for coal traffic. Of these no fewer than 1,172 received no traffic at all, in a full calendar year! Beeching commented that although 'open' it was clear many of these yards had fallen into disuse. A further 1,790 station yards (that is 36 per cent of the total) received between one and five wagons per week. At the other end of the scale, 64 stations received over 50,000 tons of coal per year or 20 per cent of the total coal flow.

All the coal from these stations had to be distributed by road with an average road journey of 2.5 miles. Instead of over 5,000 coal yards it was calculated that the whole country could be covered by an average 10-mile radius if there were to be just 250 distribution centres. It was calculated that the cost of delivering coal in the suggested configuration would be reduced by over 30 per cent. It was also stated that these proposals would benefit the railways, the NCB and the consumer. The recommendation was to accelerate the creation of 'coal concentration depots' and for these depots to be sold to and developed by private enterprise.

Although some aspects of carrying minerals by rail were similar to the coal industry, far better use was made of block trains working between depots that were geared-up to quickly handle the rail traffic. The industry was held up as a shining light with a comment that the through train block loads, fast handling and lower unit costs should be the aim of the coal industry. As regards wagonload and general merchandise traffic the picture was very bleak indeed, although a clear distinction was made between siding-to-siding traffic and that which involved any sort of road collection or delivery using railway-owned road vehicles.

Most importantly, the railways were having to handle poor loading traffic that road hauliers would reject or carry only at a very high price. The obvious was pointed

▼ More than 700 War Department 2-8-0 freight engines were taken into BR stock and they helped the railways get out of what would have been a post-war jam by performing herculean tasks over many years, undertaking the least glamorous duties on the BR system. They were never cleaned and the only shiny examples were ex-works. About to pass Calder Bridge signalbox in the proximity of Wakefield motive power depot, is No 90482 on 12 May 1966 with a typical train of coal empties making for a nearby colliery. *Author*

out, that there were financial advantages in BR carrying heavier loads (more wagons) over longer distances. Even with the preferred siding-to-siding traffic there were wide discrepancies in usage. For example, 78 per cent of traffic flowed to 855 sidings whereas a further 5,039 sidings handled only 22 per cent of total volumes. There was a direct correlation in costs between siding usage and overall tonnage, the low tonnage and therefore little-used siding being uneconomic and heavily loss making (but not as much as with rail-to-road trans-shipment).

Much time and space was given to justifying the closure of minor stations, yards and sidings because volumes were low and unit costs were high. Low traffic figures meant that only a small number of businesses would be affected if such installations were closed. Much of the traffic was 'bad' traffic but little would be saved unless total closure took place because 'it would serve little purpose to thin out the traffic without closing the stations'. The heavy-cost items that were best eliminated were road collection and delivery, trip working, terminal expenses, marshalling, provision of wagons (for often small loads), trunk haulage and paper documentation.

Beeching and his colleagues spent a considerable amount of time analysing the various types of wagonload and merchandise traffic but there were few areas where there was enormous potential for profit making in haulage by rail. Much was predicated by the amount of effort, time and cost that private companies were prepared to sponsor, but it was noted that there had been a shortfall in BR's selling effort and that more 'vigorous selling' was called for, especially in the area of potential block train and siding-to-siding traffic.

One chink of light was the possibility of developing a 'Liner Train' network. Although broadly similar principles had been adopted in some other countries the British Railways Board was, in UK terms, thinking that perhaps in the future, such a mode of operation would prove enormously successful, albeit in a modified format, particularly in respect of longer distance domestic and international traffic. The idea was to combine rail and road movements in such a way as to take advantage of the lower cost of fast through-train movement as a means of providing trunk haulage over medium to long distances. This particularly applied to dense flows of traffic that individually were too small in themselves to justify through-train operation, without the disadvantages of either costly assembly of trains by wagonload movement on rail, or costly transfer of merchandise between road and rail trailers. The method for this was to link main centres of industry and population by services of fast, regular-scheduled, through trains.

These trains would be comprised of specially designed, permanently coupled, low flat wagons capable of taking large containers of the newly recommended international 8ft by 8ft dimensions with the length of modules being either 10, 20 or 30ft. These containers would be transferred to and from flat-decked road vehicles, for back loads. Amusingly, one of the benefits of the system was claimed to be 'freedom from pilferage'! The BRB saw this mode of operation as being fast, relatively cheap, reliable, simple with less documentation, easy loading and the elimination of both marshalling and double handling (from a railway perspective). The proposal was for 55 such terminals. The total cost would be in the region of £100 million but an annual profit, described as a contribution, of £18 million was envisaged, compared with a then existing net deficit for that type of traffic of £31.8 million. This proposal was as near to the existing freightliner and intermodal system as one could imagine (with far more terminals), but largely for domestic use.

As regards the freight sundries traffic that BR was burdened with, their traditional obligations under common carrier legislation prevailed and there was little that the railways were not legally obliged or able to carry. This was contrary to the business practices of those providing road services who selected only good and profitable traffic. This source of traffic suffered such huge losses that it was difficult to make suggestions that would change the balance sheet from red to black. If the thousands of stations and points where such traffic could be handled was reduced to just 100 and the cost of transit was modified to accurately reflect the true cost of carriage, it was thought that there might be scope for generating profitable income. However, after making a series of suggestions as to how such traffic could be handled profitably there was a 'throw-away' phrase in the report, which clearly stated that whatever changes were made, some of them involving capital costs, that such traffic was 'particularly unattractive'. Reading between the lines it is clear that BR would rather have dispensed in total with sundries and small volume goods, which was an operational pain in the neck and a financial liability.

Slowly but surely progress was made during the late 1960s and early 1970s, especially with the introduction of diesel and electric traction and in the modernisation of the wagon fleet. The total BR wagon fleet had already been reduced from 1,252,000 in 1946 to 848,591 (how's that for detail!) in 1963, but further significant inroads were subsequently made. The 1963 Reshaping Report stated that a further 100,000 wagons would be withdrawn in the current year and a provisional and conservative target would see the fleet reduced to 500,000 wagons. Steam finally disappeared and branch and minor line closures continued apace, reducing costs but also goods and freight volume and therefore gross income. Although more detail will follow, in 1952 BR carried a grand total of 289 million tons of freight. Four years after Beeching's Reshaping Report, in 1967, the railways carried 204 million tons; in 1982 the total was 141.9 million tons, and towards the end of BR operations in 1996, 101.7 million tons, little more than one-third of the tonnage carried 44 years earlier!

1950s AND 1960s IN ACTION

▲ It was not always the case of a dirty freight steam locomotive working non-passenger trains. In this case one of BR Western Region's gleaming 'Castle' class 4-6-0s, No 5053 *Earl Cairns*, passes Baldhu, west of Truro, with an up perishables train from Penzance on 24 September 1961. The amount of seasonal produce once sent by rail out of Cornwall was remarkable. For example, in 1937 a total of 70 special trains left the county containing 55,000 tons of broccoli. Flowers were another speciality when early spring blooms were speedily despatched by rail to London in special trains. All that is now history. *Les Elsey*

▼ For goods trains that ran over shorter distances every one of the pre-Nationalisation railway companies had classes of freight tank engines. Some were quite powerful such as the chunky 81-ton 3100 class 2-6-2Ts, seen here, which had a broadly similar power output to a 'Castle' class 4-6-0. These locomotives were a Collett rebuild of an earlier Churchward design but with a higher boiler pressure and smaller wheels. No 3102 is seen approaching Wolverhampton Low Level with a goods for Wrexham on 17 July 1954. *Brian Morrison*

▲ One of the problems encountered by BR in its early days was pathing goods and freight trains on passenger routes. In stark contrast to the current scene most of the goods trains depicted here were restricted to 40–45mph, due to short-wheelbase wagons, a variety of braking systems and the capability of the motive power. Heading east from Wellington, Salop on 30 August 1952 is Collett '2251' class 0-6-0 No 2279 with a Chester to Wolverhampton wagonload freight. *Brian Morrison*

▼ This scene illustrates where BR lost most of its money, by running hopelessly loss-making services at an unrealistic cost level, often under its common carrier obligations. Looking like a scene from the *Titfield Thunderbolt* film 0-4-2T No 5818 runs into the small platform at Dorstone station on the backwater from Pontrilas, between Abergavenny and Hereford, to Hay on 21 June 1951. The line was a wartime casualty for passenger trains, closing in December 1941, but it struggled on for freight until 1953. *W.A. Camwell/SLS*

▶ A wonderful impression of steam power as former GWR 2-8-0 No 3817 of Cardiff Canton depot blasts its way up Hatton Bank on 6 November 1956, banked by a 5100 class 2-6-2T. The heavy load of iron ore is working from Banbury to Bilston, north-west of Birmingham. Another feature of the BR of yesteryear is the line of tall telegraph poles on the right supporting some two dozen individual wires. *Michael Mensing*

▼ The photographer recorded this pleasant scene at 2.53pm on 20 September 1958, which accords with the time shown on the church tower clock at West Bromwich. Heading east with an up freight, 0-6-0 pannier tank No 9753 has a respectable load of 16 wagons and a brake van behind it. By this time the Modernisation Plan was being implemented and it was clear that within a decade of this date the last fire in a BR steam locomotive's firebox would be extinguished. *Michael Mensing*

▶ Photographically Britain's second city of Birmingham is often poorly represented in railway books, a situation hereby redressed. However, by implication there has always been a comprehensive freight network surrounding the city, of both London & North Western Railway and Great Western Railway origins. Firmly in former GWR territory is trusty Mogul 2-6-0 No 7317 seen with a down freight on the main line from Snow Hill at Priestfield station, on 30 April 1960. The lines to the right go to Dudley and beyond. *Michael Mensing*

▶ One of the rail routes that saw regular freight on a Sunday was between Worcester and Hereford, a main artery between South Wales and the Midlands. Heavy, 92-ton 7200 class 2-8-2T No 7251 heads a down rake of empty 20-ton coke wagons on the approach to Colwall Tunnel under the Malvern Hills, on 19 June 1960. These locomotives were Collett rebuilds of the 4200 class 2-8-0Ts with an added pair of trailing wheels and extended coal bunkers. *Michael Mensing*

▶ One of the joys of platform-end train spotting or photography in the 'old days' was not knowing what was going to come around the corner next, especially at Bristol Temple Meads. On 28 September 1959, 5600 class 0-6-2T No 6630 trundles into the station with a commendable load. These locomotives were originally built for service in the Welsh Valleys. By this time diesel locomotives were being delivered in ever-increasing numbers, although many early types would not be as reliable as this Collett product from 1927. *Michael Mensing*

▲ In this fascinating June 1961 scene from mid-Cornwall both the main line freight and the branch goods are of a similar length, but that is where the similarity ends. Rolling down the steeply graded Drinnick Mill branch and arriving at Burngullow is 0-6-0PT No 3790, which will end up in St Blazey Yard after reversing at Par. On the up main line 'Grange' class 4-6-0 No 6869 *Resolven Grange* has come up from Truro with its lightweight load and it has a clear road to St Austell. The 'Grange' class were useful mixed traffic locomotives and the Cornish crews preferred their smaller driving wheel characteristics compared with the 'Hall' class. *W.A. Camwell/SLS*

▼ The timetable on the former Cambrian Railways line through Caersws was infrequent enough to allow the local freight to indulge in a little leisurely shunting. The station was once the junction for the Van branch, a mineral line that was open between 1871 and 1940. Shunting a horsebox in the mid-1950s is one of the 9000 class 'Dukedogs'. This nickname was derived from these 4-4-0s being a rebuild combining 'Duke' class boilers and 'Bulldog' class frames. The locomotives were regulars on the line because their useful route availability allowed them to work across the weight-restricted lines, particularly Barmouth Bridge. *W.A. Camwell/SLS*

▶ The operators have correctly matched a GWR heavy freight 2-8-0 with a goods train that is so long it disappears from view. Passing Aynho Junction south of Banbury with a down train on 29 August 1962 is No 2826, while in the opposite direction, Class 52 No D1035 *Western Yeoman* rushes by with the 11.40 Birkenhead to Paddington express. The single track on the right is the down connection from the High Wycombe and Bicester route. The third, fourth and fifth wagons are ESSO fuel tankers that originated at Fawley in Hampshire. *Michael Mensing*

▶ Pounding out of the Severn Tunnel with competing staccato beats, 5101 class 'Prairie' 2-6-2T No 4119 pilots 4200 class 2-8-0T No 4289 as they head towards Pilning with a lengthy 46-wagon freight from Severn Tunnel Junction on 9 May 1958. Such a train would require at least eight minutes to negotiate the 4-mile 628-yard tunnel and so it was a good job that such a working preceded the era of the High Speed Train. The train has already been switched to the up slow line. *Michael Mensing*

▶ In appalling external condition, with depot staff no doubt of the opinion that there was little point in cleaning a locomotive that would shortly be doomed and destined for the scrap heap, 4200 class No 4235 clanks through Cardiff General station on 20 April 1962 with a down freight. One wonders how many different final destinations there would be for the four-wheeled period pieces behind the 2-8-0T. By this time work on Dr Richard Beeching's Reshaping Plan was well under way, which would be the death knell of such workings. *Michael Mensing*

▲ In addition to goods and freight trains, over the decades BR ran scores of parcels and newspaper trains every day of the week on every region of their network. However, towards the end of the 50-year era much of this rail traffic had been lost, it being either uneconomic or in the case of the newspapers costly, inflexible and unreliable compared with road transport. This was not the case on 13 July 1951 when D1 class 4-4-0 No 31741 was photographed on the Chislehurst Loop heading towards St Mary Cray with a London Bridge to Dover parcels train. *Brian Morrison*

▼ The South Eastern & Chatham Railway's version of the popular freight 0-6-0 was the Wainwright C class of 1900. They were not particularly powerful, being classified only in the 2F category by BR. Working hard and darkening the Kentish skies is No 31724, seen heading a freight bound for Dover, via Maidstone East, at Chislehurst, also on 13 July 1951. The leading van has 'LMS' painted on its side giving a clue that some of the wagons will have travelled from the north-west of the Metropolis. *Brian Morrison*

▲ One of the oldest standard gauge railways in the UK was the famous Canterbury & Whitstable Railway. The line was opened in 1830 and connected Canterbury West with the harbour at Whitstable. The line had a very limited clearance as strikingly seen in the case of this tunnel. This resulted in locomotives with specially fitted short chimneys and cut-down cabs working the line. One such example was R1 class 0-6-0T No 31339 (as well as Nos 31010 and 31147), seen here in BR's early days. The line closed to passengers way back in January 1931, and to goods traffic from March 1953. *SLS*

▼ Beauty is, they say, in the eye of the beholder but in the case of this 4P5F mixed traffic former London & South Western Railway H15 class 4-6-0 a tiny squat chimney sitting on top of a large diameter smokebox looks somewhat incongruous. Nos 30330–30334 were Maunsell rebuilds of earlier Drummond locomotives. No 30334 works through Worting Junction, near Basingstoke, on 8 September 1952 with down empty hoppers. The lines on the right and high up on the left are the down and up roads to Southampton, whereas the freight is on the Salisbury and Exeter route. *Brian Morrison*

▲ The Southern's Q1 class 0-6-0s were distinctive in every respect, earning the class a range of nicknames. They were a wartime product of so-called 'austerity' design from the drawing board of O.V.S. Bulleid. They were powerful for their size and efforts were made in their design to ease maintenance. Sporting its Bulleid-pattern driving wheels, No 33020 (cleaned to show only its former Southern Railway number of C20) passes one of the yards at Guildford as it makes for the shed in January 1965. Although primarily freight engines, towards the end of their careers they could often be found working Reading to Redhill passenger trains. *Author*

▼ Swept away years ago and now beyond the memory of many was Reading's 'Southern' station, or Reading South to be more accurate. The station was adjacent to its more illustrious Western Region neighbour. There was a reasonable volume of parcels traffic handled at the station, mainly to a Post Office depot at Redhill, but also to Dover. In this 1960s view U class 2-6-0 No 31799 heads just three vans. The station closed in September 1965 when all traffic was diverted to its larger WR neighbour. *W.A. Camwell/SLS*

▲ How the mighty have fallen, as one of Bulleid's 'West Country' class Pacific locomotives is relegated to humble freight duty during its dying days. A few days earlier, No 34102 *Lapford* (although here de-named) had been employed on a Waterloo to Bournemouth express but here, in May 1966, it heads a down fitted freight at Winchester. The train will almost certainly recess at Eastleigh, a few miles to the south. The third rail is already in situ for the forthcoming electrification of the route. *Author*

▼ Most enthusiasts associate coal with either South Wales, Scotland, South Yorkshire or the Nottinghamshire/Derbyshire areas. What is not so well known is that for many years a large number of collieries operated in the county of Kent, with Betteshanger, Tilmanstone, Snowdown and Chislet being the longest survivors. The last of these closed in 1989. The conversion of the railways from steam to diesel and electric power and the installation of gas-fired central heating in millions of households impacted the customer base to a considerable extent. On 20 February 1953 N class 2-6-0 No 31404 is seen on the Chislehurst Loop with a load of coal from the Kentish pits, contained in wooden-sided wagons. *Brian Morrison*

◀ One of the most famous lines in the UK was the old Somerset & Dorset Joint Railway, which ran from Bath Green Park to Broadstone Junction, with services continuing to Bournemouth West. There were also a number of branches to Highbridge, Bridgwater, Wells and Wimborne. Leaving Devonshire Tunnel, Bath, on 13 May 1964 is Stanier 8F No 48737 with a southbound freight, which was being banked by pannier tank No 3742. The 2-8-0 freight engines had then recently replaced the purpose-built ex-Midland Railway Fowler 7F class 2-8-0s numbered in the 53800 to 53810 series. The entire route closed in March 1966 except for a couple of freight-only stubs. *Michael Mensing*

▶ Another delightful branch freight is featured here but this time north of the border. Running tender first along the Kirkcudbright branch with an up goods train for the junction at Castle Douglas is 5MT 4-6-0 No 44957 on 19 July 1963, a task well within the capabilities of such a large locomotive. Passenger services were withdrawn in May 1965 and goods services went the same way the following month, relegating scenes such as this to railway history. *Michael Mensing*

◀ When our intrepid photographer fought his way to this spot between Middle and South Harecastle tunnels in September 1960 he was not to know that within a decade the BBC would screen what would become a famous 'Wednesday Play' called *The Last Train Through Harecastle Tunnel*. The 1969 production was directed by Alan Clarke and starred John Le Mesurier. Leaving the tunnel, situated between Kidsgrove and Stoke-on-Trent, with an up train of limestone hoppers is 4F 0-6-0 No 44352. *Michael Mensing*

► Two of the all-time classic London & North Western Railway heavy freight engines were the 'Super D' class G1 and G2 0-8-0 locomotives, dating from 1914 and 1921 and rated at 6F and 7F respectively. Many of the class were later rebuilt with Belpaire boilers and a higher boiler pressure. Seen south of Foleshill on the Coventry to Nuneaton line with a northbound freight on 24 June 1961, is G2 No 49439. While the sidings are partly weed covered they are still populated by a handful of wagons. *Michael Mensing*

◄ It must have made the photographer's day to capture on film one of Fowler's LMS 'Patriot' class 4-6-0s on freight duty on 29 April 1958. Unnamed example No 45510 hammers away from Rugby on the Trent Valley line with a down express freight, with 'Door to Door' containers to the fore. None of the class was preserved but a new-build project for one of these three-cylinder locomotives, which had their origins in the LNWR 'Claughton' class, is now under way. *Michael Mensing*

► Looking almost like a runaway train, 4F class 0-6-0 No 44226, a Saltley Birmingham engine, storms through Bromsgrove station with the benefit of a 1-in-37 downgrade behind it, on 20 April 1957. Although the fitted freight train would be restricted to about 40mph, a burst of the regulator gives the impression of even greater speed. The grimy brickwork and the attached gas lamp were typical of the era. *Michael Mensing*

▲ The complexity of the trackwork is rivalled only by the 46 semaphore signals that can be seen in this view just south of Preston station. On a foul 17 April 1968 grimy 8F No 48476 plods through the rain with a freight, largely comprising sheeted wagons to keep out the elements. The end of steam operation was just weeks away and, soon, a 138-year era would come to an end. The nearby Lostock Hall motive power depot was still open, the last in the immediate area. *Author*

▼ Goods and freight services are not only about branch and main line running. Every wagon has to be loaded and unloaded, whether it be in a goods yard or the major industrial premises of a rail freight customer. In the case of the latter a shunter was sometimes provided, either by BR or the customer. This photograph shows the scene at Staveley Iron and Steel Works in 1964 as BR 0-4-0 saddle tank No 47005 arranges some local wagons. Originally built for the LMS by Kitson in 1932, this particular locomotive was rebuilt at Horwich Works in 1953 with extended saddle tanks and an increased coal capacity. It was withdrawn in 1966. *Gavin Morrison*

▲ Absolutely oozing with atmosphere and reflecting the grime associated with the steam age, particularly the blackened signalbox on the left, is this scene at Bolton Trinity Street on 18 April 1968. Leaving the depths of the station and passing upper quadrant signals with a lengthy down goods is 'Black Five' No 45104. Looking at the long lines of wagons on the right one wonders in retrospect how the businesses and tradespeople of Bolton now survive without the freight-carrying railway. No doubt every commodity is now delivered by road. *Author*

▼ One also wonders whether the likes of the late Fred Dibnah, who incidentally was born in Bolton (see previous picture), was subsequently hired to fell these icons of the Industrial Revolution? Passing a fine pair of chimneys just west of Gannow Junction near Rose Grove with a lengthy parcels train that has just come off the Skipton line, is 5MT No 44809 in April 1968. The vans are of GWR, LMS, SR and BR origins. *Author*

▲ Another old timer, in this case 1875-built Johnson-designed ex-Midland Railway 2F 0-6-0 No 58229, clanks its way past West Hampstead with sheeted mineral wagons on 12 April 1952. The wagon covers were attached by rubber cleats that were hooked onto the wagons for protection of the payload. There is a rolled-up tarpaulin cover on the cab roof, which would be lowered towards the tender in bad weather to afford at least some protection to the footplate crew. *Brian Morrison*

▼ One of the purposeful Ivatt 4MT 2-6-0 Moguls, Tebay-allocated No 43009, heads the local pick-up goods past Shap Summit and prepares for its imminent descent, on 24 August 1963. The summit signalbox and the up and down loops can be seen in the left background. A total of 162 locomotives of this type were introduced from 1947. It is now hard to imagine sights such as this as 'Pendolino' units rush by at three-figure speeds. *Gavin Morrison*

▶ This train has had engineers' occupation of the Leamington to Coventry line but its work is now done and the ensemble is passing Kenilworth Junction as it returns to Coventry along the single line at 5.59pm, on 29 April 1962. Saltley's 8F No 48559 chuffs away from the site, the signalman having just handed over the single-line token to the driver. The freight-only line on the right goes to Berkswell Junction, which closed to passengers in 1965 and completely in January 1969. *Michael Mensing*

▼ The downturn in goods and freight traffic over the years has affected Scotland as much as anywhere else and on many of the lines that have survived there is now no freight traffic whatsoever. Certainly this Oban-bound goods is a thing of the past, as Stanier 5MT No 44881 was photographed about a mile west of Loch Awe on 15 May 1961. The three leading wagons are 'Presflos' containing cement and the following two box vans both have ventilators, suggesting a payload of produce or foodstuffs. *Michael Mensing*

▲ In modern times weedkilling trains comprise either self-propelled units with integral chemical/water tanks, or a set of tankers that travel the country in push-pull mode with a locomotive at each end. This is necessary because at many locations track work has been rationalised, including the removal of facilities for a single locomotive to run round its train. However, back in April 1962 such workings comprised a single locomotive and often old locomotive tenders, in which the weedkilling liquids were stored. With a brake van at each end and a Gresley coach and three tenders in the consist, 'Crab' 2-6-0 No 42795 passes remarkable signals at Morley Junction, between Keighley and Bingley, running tender first. *Gavin Morrison*

▼ Not many enthusiasts will have heard of Edzell station, north of Brechin, the terminus of an old Caledonian Railway branch line. This remote line closed to passengers in April 1931 but curiously reopened for a few weeks in 1938, before closing again. Goods services continued until September 1953 but the infrequent trains were rarely photographed. Caught on film just before closure, this wonderful record of a dying breed, Caley 0-4-4T No 55193, has four museum pieces in tow at Edzell terminus. *W.A. Camwell/SLS*

▲ An old Ford Anglia and a VW Beetle will soon be overtaking this heavy and slow-moving freight east of Todmorden on 18 May 1968. The road, railway, river and canal all have to fit in this narrow section of the Calder Valley. Class 8F No 48410 heads west with a coal train travelling from Yorkshire to Lancashire over the viaducts between Horsfall and Millwood tunnels. The train would take the Copy Pit line where banking assistance would be necessary from Hall Royd Junction to the summit. *Gavin Morrison*

▼ For much of the day Killin Junction on the now-closed line from Dunblane to Crianlarich was a sleepy hollow, but in this view it looks like a train spotters' paradise. With 'British Railways' painted on the tender a freight is headed by 4-6-0 No 44995, while to the left of the tall ex-Caledonian Railway signal, another 'Black Five' heads a passenger train. In the island platform is the Killin branch train. The line closed in 1965 following a serious landslip. *SLS*

◀ The Gresley-designed LNER V2 class of 2-6-2s were good all-rounders and were equally at home on fast freights or anything other than the very top link of express passenger trains. A handful of the 184 locomotives were named, such as No 60873 *Coldstreamer* seen here working an up fast fitted freight on the East Coast Main Line, near to the Anglo/Scottish border, north of Berwick-upon-Tweed on 30 May 1962. The train would almost certainly have originated in Millerhill Yard, Edinburgh, and would no doubt pause for breath at Tyne Yard south of Newcastle upon Tyne. *Michael Mensing*

◀ The Class O1 2-8-0s were the Great Central Railway's primary heavy freight engine that was first introduced to a Robinson design in 1911. However, over the years an immense number of modifications were made, resulting in the creation of a Class O4 development. Changes took place in 1917, 1924/25, 1932, 1939 and 1944 and over 300 locomotives in total were placed in either the 7F or 8F category. This 1944 rebuild, No 63803, is seen powering along the former Great Central main line about half a mile south of Rugby Central with an up freight, on 7 November 1956. *Michael Mensing*

◀ Just a glimpse of a bridge over the River Tyne can be seen above the awnings of Manors station, Newcastle upon Tyne. Leaving the Jesmond line with up 20-ton coal hoppers is ex-North Eastern Railway G6 class 0-8-0 No 63458. Although there is some through freight in the Tyneside area on the north–south axis and block loads ranging from oil to imported coal and aluminium make regular incursions, no marshalling now takes place in Tyne Yard and the frenetic activity of times past has gone for ever. *Michael Mensing*

▶ Judges would give the driver of J27 class No 65788 ten out of ten for effort as the venerable machine pounds up the 1 in 133 from Rhyhope Grange Junction with empties for reloading at the now long-closed Silksworth Colliery on 10 May 1966. In those days it was possible to get a lineside pass from Regional Headquarters and so 'wrong side of the fence' photography was in order. In most cases the views from non-railway land were just as good and sometimes better! *Author*

▼ One of the most remarkable freight locomotives ever to work on BR metals, but one that over the years has received scant publicity, was the vast 178-ton Gresley/Beyer Peacock 2-8-8-2 Beyer-Garratt of 1925. This machine had a tractive effort equivalent to three 4F 0-6-0s, two and a quarter 8F 2-8-0s, or two Gresley A4 Pacifics. In the 1950s it could often be found at work on the Woodhead route where its power on trans-Pennine freight traffic was exploited. In this 1950s scene at Crowden west of Woodhead the one-off No 69999 appears to have paused with the footplate crew apparently in contact with the train guard. *N.R. Knight/SLS*

▲ Buchlyvie Junction in Stirlingshire was located on the line from Balloch to Stirling. Another line from Lenzie joined the route at Gartness and trains from that direction mostly ran through to the terminus of the Aberfoyle branch. Passenger trains on the through route were withdrawn way back in 1934 but services from Lenzie, via Buchlyvie Junction to Aberfoyle, continued until October 1951. Passing the abandoned station and the North British Railway signalbox is K2 class 2-6-0 No 61787 *Loch Quoich* with the four-wagon branch goods; a classic example of such services targeted by Dr Beeching. It would appear to be many years since the 'Gentlemen' facilities on the left have been used, and the condition of the passing loop needs little comment! *W.A. Camwell/SLS*

▼ In this feast of photographs of remote branch goods trains we see the very last goods train to pick up at Allendale, the terminus of a branch line that ran south from Border Counties Junction, Hexham, on the Newcastle to Carlisle line. The branch closed to passenger trains on 22 September 1930, during the Great Depression, but it struggled on for goods traffic until November 1950. On 12 November of that year, 1886-built J21 class No 65082 has just three wagons coupled between the brake vans as it says its final farewells. *W.A. Camwell/SLS*

▲ Few enthusiasts will have seen photographs of the occasional goods train that ran from Melmerby North, on the now-closed Harrogate to Northallerton via Ripon line, to the outpost of Masham in North Yorkshire, which had a population of 980 in 1901. This charming scene was recorded in July 1959 and shows J39 0-6-0 No 64845 pulling forward at the terminus. Note the unusual inclined siding behind the signalbox on the left and the portly goods agent with flat cap! The line finally closed to all traffic in November 1963. *W.A. Camwell/SLS*

▼ Dramatic contrasts at Alne on the East Coast main line. As J71 class 0-6-0T No 68294 fusses with an odd assortment of wagons and stock bound for the terminus at Easingwold, a Gresley A3 class Pacific thunders through the station site on a northbound express from King's Cross. The Easingwold branch closed to passengers in November 1948 but goods traffic continued until December 1957. The Worsdell design of the tank engine dated back to 1886, typical of much ancient machinery inherited by BR in 1948. *W.A. Camwell/SLS*

▲ The 58-ton Class J50 0-6-0s could be seen in the London area on transfer freights. This example, No 68949, was one of the J50/3 subclass, a 1926 post-Grouping development of the original specification. This mixed load is descending Holloway Bank on 11 May 1953 with a working to King's Cross goods depot. Trolleybus wires over the road above date the picture. *Brian Morrison*

▼ With coal piled high in the tender of J27 No 65788 and equally high in the trailing 20-ton hopper wagons, this train from Silksworth Colliery has the road down to Rhyhope Grange Junction on 11 May 1966. The driver with a flat hat and a 'roll-up' to smoke spots the photographer as he gets the right away from the signalman on his way to the staithes. One wonders what size the congregation might be at the distant church, especially after the destruction of the mining communities. *Author*

▲ In today's world most UK railway enthusiasts interested in goods and freight trains are 'clued-up' on the identity of workings. By way of example, train 6H21 is the 08.03 Hindlow to Buxton and 6E71 is the Mossend to West Burton. However, in earlier decades wagonload goods trains comprised workings from one marshalling yard to another, or a trip working from a marshalling yard to an individual customer or specific branch line and precise train identity was difficult to ascertain. An unidentified transfer goods passes Sneinton Junction near Nottingham in the 1950s with a working that is probably bound for Colwick, behind J52 class 0-6-0ST No 68781. *J.F. Henton/SLS*

▼ More wonderful railway infrastructure of yesteryear finds rare bird V4 class 2-6-2 No 61701 departing from Aberdeen with the 6.25am pick-up goods for Laurencekirk to the south, on 26 June 1957. Introduced by Gresley in 1941, just before he died, there were only two locomotives of the class built as his successor Thompson concentrated on the B1 class 4-6-0s. The locomotive's shed allocation of Aberdeen Ferryhill has been painted on the bufferbeam, but later in the year both examples were withdrawn as boiler certificates ran out. *Brian Morrison*

▶ It was not every day that one of Gresley's streamlined A4 class Pacifics worked a freight train, but on 7 July 1962 Gateshead's No 60001 *Sir Ronald Matthews* was entrusted with an up express fitted freight, seen climbing to the southern portal of Stoke Tunnel. At this time the last of the 22-strong 3,300hp 'Deltic' fleet of diesel-electric locomotives had just been delivered, resulting in some A4s being surplus to requirements on passenger workings. *Gavin Morrison*

▼ In current times UK railway enthusiasts pursuing and photographing freight trains are likely to find a Class 66 variant on the point, with a lesser chance of perhaps a Class 60 or 70, but in times past variety was truly the spice of life with hundreds of different classes of steam locomotive to be seen nationwide. It was one of Raven's 1920-built B16/1 class 4-6-0s that greeted the photographer at Doncaster on 31 August 1954, as No 61460 headed south. *Brian Morrison*

▲ Another B16 class is featured here, but one of the B16/3 subclass, a 1944 variant by Thompson featuring Walschaerts valve gear. No 61439 rushes through Pilmoor, between York and Darlington, in 1959 with a respectable load containing the usual, seemingly infinite, variety of four-wheeled wagons, in this case vacuum fitted. *Gavin Morrison*

▼ There is little doubt that the crew of this O2 class 2-8-0 will appreciate running tender first into Stoke Tunnel south of Grantham on the East Coast Main Line so that smoke and steam will be carried towards the rear of the train rather than into the cab. Hauling wagons of the era, which nowadays would look more at home on a modeller's layout, No 63932 must keep to schedule on this two-track section so as not to delay following express passenger trains. *Gavin Morrison*

▲ In 1949, BR had a staggering 1,165,000 wagons on its network, many of them of considerable vintage and obsolete even by the then current standards. By getting close to the action the photographer has demonstrated just how dilapidated some goods vehicles were, including the foreground 'Hybar' wagons. The scene is the junction of Battersby, where trains on the Esk Valley route still have to reverse on their journey from Middlesbrough to Whitby. On 28 July 1958, a goods from the now-closed Picton line is headed by Fairburn 2-6-4T No 42085 (now preserved on the Lakeside & Haverthwaite Railway), while on the left is the local diesel multiple unit. The destination boards are a wonderful touch. *Michael Mensing*

▼ Stripped of its *Tennyson* nameplates 'Britannia' class 4-6-0 No 70032 makes music in the hills on 1 April 1967 as it works hard while making its way through the Lune Gorge to Tebay, where banking assistance will be attached. In the last few years of steam nearly all of the class were allocated to Carlisle Kingmoor, where the 'Brits' were mainly given freight duties. Modern welded flat-bottomed rail on concrete sleepers is beginning to make an appearance. *Gavin Morrison*

▲ This superb impression of steam, smoke and power shows BR Class 9F 2-10-0 No. 92120 recovering from a signal check at Knowle & Dorridge station on the former GWR Leamington to Birmingham route, at 6.55pm on 14 August 1959, with a down freight. Introduced from 1954 the class was to become BR's version of a heavy freight locomotive but by the time the last of the 251-strong class was delivered in 1960 steam was doomed and many had working lives of only six or seven years. *Michael Mensing*

▼ A total of ten Class 9F locomotives were allocated to Tyne Dock shed to work the iron ore trains up to the steel works at Consett. They were fitted with Westinghouse air pumps to operate the wagon doors when discharging their loads. The 9Fs replaced older Class O1 and Q7 locomotives but they too would cease working such trains on 19 November 1966. These very heavy trains were banked up the steep gradient, which in places was 1 in 51. On 18 March 1966 No 92099 is helped by WD 2-8-0 No 90434 as the pair blast past Stanley, County Durham. *Gavin Morrison*

▲ Passing tenement blocks near Polmadie that were typical of those found in many areas of suburban Glasgow, is standard 'Clan' class 4-6-2 No 72003 *Clan Fraser* with a down freight, on 27 June 1957. Only ten of the class were built, from 1952, although train spotting books of the mid-1950s show a list of 24 locomotives, all with names, and a note that 'engines of this class are still being delivered'. There were stories that the class did not steam well but decades later the source of such claims seems unclear. A dedicated group are trying to produce a 'new-build' Clan, finance as always being a problem. *Brian Morrison*

▼ Stainmore was a truly remote spot located near the summit of the old North Eastern Railway route from Appleby and Kirkby Stephen to Barnard Castle and Darlington or West Auckland, which closed to passengers in stages between 1962 and 1964. The North Eastern Region of BR had an allocation of ten BR Standard 2-6-0s in the 780xx series and these were shared between Northallerton and Kirkby Stephen motive power depots. Consequently they were much used on the above-mentioned line. Having tackled the formidable climb from Kirkby Stephen to Stainmore Summit, which included crossing the famous Belah Viaduct, Nos 78017 and 78013 are seen leaving the summit area for West Auckland, the former engine having acted as banker until reaching this point. *Gavin Morrison*

▲ As a variant of the BR Standard Class 9F 2-10-0, Nos 92020 to 92029 were fitted with Franco-Crosti boilers, a novel design of Italian origin. Although efficient there were operational problems that demolished the case for retention, all locomotives being converted to a more conventional configuration at a later date. A converted No 92029 approaches Bentley Heath, near Knowle & Dorridge, with an up coal train on 16 June 1964. *Michael Mensing*

▶ Contravening the conditions of the 1956 and 1968 Clean Air Acts is WD 2-8-0 No 90370 as it darkens the sky over the River Calder Bridge near Wakefield Kirkgate with a coal train in May 1966. At the time of Nationalisation coal comprised 58 per cent of the total goods and freight carried by BR, but over the years this gradually declined as the use of both domestic and industrial coal diminished in favour of other energy sources. *Author*

▲ Back in 1961, Weymouth could still boast a goods service, routed over both Southern Region lines towards Southampton and on Western Region metals from Dorchester West. In striking lined-black livery BR Standard Class 5MT 4-6-0 No 73117 *Vivien* leaves the seaside town and it will try to quickly build up speed to tackle the steep climb to Upwey. Twenty of these locomotives based on the Southern Region had names from withdrawn 'King Arthur' class 4-6-0s applied, the plates being fitted to the side of the running plate. *Michael Mensing*

▼ In stark contrast with the previous picture, No 73158 could not be in more deplorable condition as it approaches Wakefield Kirkgate with a 15-wagon freight making its way from the Normanton direction to Healey Mills on 12 May 1966. Somebody has stolen the smokebox number plate, which will no doubt find its way into a private collection rather than be found at a public auction, where its origins may be challenged. *Author*

◄ Here we show a trio of photographs of automobiles being carried by train in the first 15 years of BR's existence. Long before the first Severn Bridge was built motorists wanting to travel from Bristol to South Wales were faced with a lengthy drive via Gloucester or a slow car ferry across the river. BR provided a special car shuttle service through the Severn Tunnel, from Severn Tunnel Junction to Pilning (High Level). Cars were initially carried on short, four-wheeled wagons and here, 6100 class 2-6-2T No 6119 hauls the 4.40pm car transporter out of the tunnel on 9 May 1958. The four cars include an Austin Westminster and a Bentley limousine. *Michael Mensing*

◄ This photograph reputedly shows the first Motorail car-carrying bogie wagons for use on the Severn Tunnel Junction to Pilning service on 14 September 1963. In this splendid nostalgic scene a Ford Popular, Wolsey 1500, Hillman Minx, Austin Mini and Morris Traveller are using the service, with not a German or Japanese car in sight. It is reassuring to see the upright Ford owner is a member of the Royal Automobile Club, which may reflect on the reliability of these now vintage vehicles. *RCTS*

► Far removed from today's enclosed or partially enclosed car carriers is this scene on the Oxford to Didcot line with an intriguing combination, incorporated in the pannier tank-headed Abingdon branch goods. Not only has general wagonload traffic been included but also an assortment of MG sports cars from its Abingdon factory. The mandatory brake van is bringing up the rear of the train. The up and down goods loops are controlled by Radley signalbox. *Author's Collection*

▲ Photographing small shunters working goods trains on a main line is an opportunity not to be missed. On 27 June 1966 Class 04 No D2288 passes Holes Bay Junction, west of Poole in Dorset, with what is thought to be a train from Hamworthy Goods. The lines to the right were once used by trains working over the Somerset & Dorset Joint Railway or to West Moors, which would continue to either Salisbury or Brockenhurst via Ringwood. *Gavin Morrison*

▼ Far removed from Dorset is this illustration of 204hp Barclay Class 06 No D2436, which is tripping through Newton-on-Ayr, between Falkland Junction and Newton Junction with down coal wagons in July 1965. The author was hunting down steam trains at the time, but fortunately used a frame on the diesel, which in retrospect is more interesting than a 'Black Five'! Built in April 1960 the little locomotive would have a life of only 11 years, being withdrawn in November 1971 and disposed of at BREL Glasgow in 1973. *Author*

▶ Although previously published, this photograph taken at the closed Fittleworth station in West Sussex is one of the author's favourite shots, mainly because at the time he was the GPO's caretaker telephone operator in the village exchange that had 157 subscribers. Simply photographing the thrice-weekly train was something of an achievement. The photographer's Villiers-engined 197cc James motorcycle can just be seen to the left of the wooden station building. Passenger services through to Midhurst ceased in 1955 and by April 1966 only the branch goods from Pulborough to Petworth survived. Within four weeks the last train would run. The Class 08 and its empty coal wagons would work through to Horsham. The station has been preserved in private hands but mature trees now cover the foreground. *Author*

▼ From the late 1950s in particular, more and more diesel locomotives were introduced and for over a decade there was an uneasy cohabitation in many areas. One of the first areas to be completely dieselised was Devon and Cornwall, but unfortunately early arrivals proved not to be the most reliable of machines. The 1,000/1,100hp Class 22s from the North British stable had a relatively short life, this example, No D6309, being delivered in January 1960 and withdrawn in May 1971. Looking to be in an uncared-for state the Type 2 diesel-hydraulic is seen in Truro Yard on 6 June 1970 with evidence of working china clay trains on the cab ends. *R.F. Roberts/SLS*

▲ Absolutely gleaming and without a yellow warning panel in sight, immaculate English Electric Type 1 No D8034 (later Class 20 No 20034) ambles along the Ballater branch in Scotland with a goods train for Aberdeen on 13 July 1964. The train is seen about three-quarters of a mile to the east of Lumphanan. Single-line tablet catching apparatus is carried, just below the running number. Train services were withdrawn in 1966, with freight continuing for a few weeks after passenger workings ceased. *Michael Mensing*

▼ The 800hp British Thomson-Houston Class 15s, as they were to become, were delivered from 1957. They were fitted with a 16-cylinder Paxman diesel engine and tipped the scales at 68 tons. Orders totalled 44 locomotives, the last tranche being built by the Clayton company. The class was successful initially, but serious engine problems beset them and to compound the situation they were considered to be non-standard under BR's 1967 National Traction Plan. All were withdrawn between 1968 and 1971. Here, No D8242 is seen on the outskirts of Ipswich on 17 August 1969 with an up freight mainly comprising cement wagons. The class mostly worked in the east London suburbs and on East Anglian branches. *John Cooper-Smith*

▲ Another motive power flop was the English Electric Napier-engined Class 23 'Baby Deltic'. The number of problems with these locomotives could fill a small book (as described in the companion volume *The Rise and Fall of British Railways: Main Line Diesel Locomotives*). Delivered from 1959 the class of ten locomotives were unreliable and at a point in time during 1963 every locomotive was out of action. Within the first 15 months of service there had been a staggering 44 engine changes. A partial rebuild did not cure all of the problems and they duly became modern traction history. On 8 October 1967 Nos D5903 and D9504 were photographed on a ballast train at Hadley Wood, 11 miles from King's Cross. *Author's Collection*

▼ By the time the Class 17s had been delivered the very work for which they were designed such as lighter freight trains, branch goods workings and transfer freights was in steep decline. Before the first locomotive had turned a wheel further orders were made, an unbelievable situation for an untried and untested machine. The first of 117 locomotives was delivered in 1962 and the first to be withdrawn was in 1968! By comparison, the English Electric Class 20s were eight times more reliable than these 900hp twin-engined centre-cab devices. Only one example was preserved, No D8568, which is seen here at Princes Risborough with a demonstration freight in April 1992. This Clayton can now be seen in action at the Chinnor & Princes Risborough Railway. *Author*

◄ Over the years engineers' or civil engineers' trains have made up a sizeable chunk of BR's non-passenger business. In fact, after privatisation Network Rail's contract, won by English Welsh & Scottish Railways, comprised a whopping 15 per cent of EWS's total gross income. In times when the entire operation came under the BR flag, all-green BR Sulzer 1,160hp Type 2 No D5051 eases out of sidings to enter New Southgate station in north London with a lengthy ballast train. Photographed on 20 January 1962. *Michael Mensing*

◄ One of BR's early ideas was to procure a large number of small Type 1 and Type 2 diesel locomotives that could work singly on lighter trains or be coupled together to work in multiple on heavier workings, rather than using what would be overpowered Type 4s. Passing Spean Bridge station on the West Highland line on 14 July 1965 is Birmingham Railway Carriage & Wagon Company Type 2 No D5355 (later Class 27 No 27009) and compatible English Electric Type 1 No D8088 (later Class 20 No 20088) with a down freight containing a number of alumina wagons for Fort William. The reason for double heading here was not only train weight but also restricted axle loading. *Michael Mensing*

◄ At many depots there was no pride whatsoever in machinery, in dramatic contrast to the pre-Grouping era when sparkling locomotives graced the railway. In shameful condition Brush Type 2, later Class 31, No D5655 passes Postland station on the abandoned March to Spalding line with up coal drag 7J93, on 28 September 1965. As delivered these locomotives were fitted with 12-cylinder 1,250hp Mirrlees engines but the class was later re-engined with more powerful and reliable 12-cylinder 1,470hp English Electric prime movers. *Michael Mensing*

▲ On occasions goods and freight trains in the 1950s and 1960s were only partially fitted in the brake department. In these cases it was even more important to calculate the available brake force. A small Sulzer in the shape of 1,250hp No D7588 (later Class 25 No 25238) heads a surprisingly long part-fitted down freight, 5M08, past Lapworth and heads towards the Birmingham area, on 24 June 1964. By this date locomotives were having small yellow warning panels painted on the cab ends. *Michael Mensing*

▼ It now seems an appalling prospect that live farm animals could be transported in these rocking four-wheeled wagons but then animal welfare has not always been at the top of the agenda, as it should be. At least these poor beasts could brag about their 'Peak' haulage. The big green 1Co-Co1 Sulzer-engined Type 4 No D86, with split headcode boxes, heads freight 5M25 through Cheltenham Spa Lansdown station on 7 July 1962 with a northbound freight. *Michael Mensing*

▲ The Southern Region's investment in the BRCW 1,550hp eight-cylinder Sulzer-engined Type 3s, later Class 33s, was a wise one and the class gained a good reputation for reliability. Although the SR did not have huge volumes of freight traffic compared with other regions (especially before the advent of the modern Freightliner), what they did have required a good middle-power-range diesel locomotive. Also in the early 1960s, the SR had a large number of non-electrified lines where a diesel replacement for steam was vital. Passing Totton west of Southampton No D6532 (eventually No 33114) heads a lengthy oil train comprising vacuum-fitted ESSO four-wheeled tankers, on 4 September 1964. *Gavin Morrison*

▼ One of the now-famous long-distance hauls for the SR Class 33s was from the Blue Circle Cement Works (previously Associated Portland Cement) at Northfleet in north Kent to Uddingston east of Glasgow in Scotland. In all-green livery No D6528 (later No 33111) is seen on the York avoiding line, adjacent to the motive power depot, on 29 May 1964, with a long train of cement tankers plus a box and brake van. The bulk of the Class 33s had a good 40-year career and a select handful saw their 50th birthday in service, in private hands. York Minster is just visible above the box van. *Gavin Morrison*

▶ The Beyer Peacock 16-cylinder Maybach-engined Type 3 B-B diesel-hydraulics packed a 1,700hp punch, which is just as well because in their early years a great deal was asked of them in passenger train terms. However, they were mixed-traffic machines and their role was hugely varied. Heading 3A03, a down van train from Paddington, and passing Old Oak Common, is No D7065 in September 1966. Although designated Class 35 the locomotives never carried numbers in the '35' series and, in any event, they were all withdrawn by 1975. Fortunately, three of the 101 examples were saved by preservationists. *P.H. Groom*

▶ This delightful train comprising a trio of old GWR-style brake vans heads south past the site of the old Hayles Abbey Halt between Honeybourne and Cheltenham on what is now part of the Gloucestershire/Warwickshire Railway (G/WR) heritage line. In charge on 15 May 1966 was 2,750hp Brush Type 4 No D1642 (later Nos 47058 and 47547) in its original, albeit work-stained, two-tone green livery with small yellow warning panel. The use of the letter 'Z' in the headcode denotes a special working. *Michael Mensing*

▶ One of the longest straight and relatively flat surviving stretches of track is from Werrington Junction, Peterborough, to Spalding. An equally straight-line route from Spalding towards Boston closed in 1970. Type 4 Co-Co No D1791 with a Class 7 empty coal train passes the 1961 closed station of Littleworth on 28 September 1965. Of special note is the operational 'somersault' semaphore signal of the old Great Northern Railway pattern. Following engine problems these big Sulzers were re-rated from 2,750hp to 2,580hp in the interests of reliability. *Michael Mensing*

▶ This most interesting photograph shows an early, complete container train from Aberdeen passing Kinnaber Junction, north-west of Montrose, on 12 July 1964 behind a fairly clean English Electric Class 40, No D361 (later No 40161). This was the precursor of today's freightliner and intermodal approach to railborne logistics and as a Class 3 working it was the highest category of freight train on the BR network; what our American cousins would call a 'hot shot'. The train would have been vacuum braked throughout in an era when air-braked trains were about to become increasingly commonplace. *Michael Mensing*

▼ English Electric 2,000hp Type 4 No D349 was one year old when photographed on 20 June 1962 traversing the delightful Aire Valley between Steeton & Silsdon and Keighley while heading towards Leeds. It would seem that the locomotive may have been used on a special or even Royal Train as silver buffers and clean bodysides were not the norm. This Class 5 freight, 5X49, is fully fitted in terms of the braking department, although the codes were changed in later years with Class 5 becoming 'empty coaching stock'. *Gavin Morrison*

▲ Although published a few years back this shot is included here because it is a good example of a green 1,750hp English Electric Type 3 running with a brake tender. These devices were heavily weighted braked rail vehicles that significantly improved the brake force and therefore braking capability of the locomotive(s) and train that they were attached to. In September 1968, No D6723 (later Class 37 No 37023) passes March East Junction and enters March station with a train of empty four-wheelers, which on trains such as 7J78 were limited to 45mph. Note the headcode lamps on the brake tender and the vacuum-brake pipe. *Author*

▼ China Clay in powdered or pelletised form is a payload that had to be protected from the elements and when loaded in open wagons tarpaulins were used to keep the substance dry. These sheets were attached by rubber cleats being hooked on to the wagons. In later years a more satisfactory arrangement was introduced with a tent-like 'hood' being fitted over a hybar. The tracks seen here through Fowey station were closed in 1968, the passenger service having been axed in 1965. A 'Warship' class diesel-hydraulic has just arrived from St Blazey for unloading at the docks, which are a few yards to the left of this scene. *R.F. Roberts/SLS*

▲ Freight flows come and go month by month and year by year; however, in November 1966 there was a curious 3.05am Bristol to Three Bridges working (although a 9G headcode signifies a Chichester–Hove–Redhill–Bricklayers Arms freight). The train was usually worked forward from Bristol to Chichester with a Class 42/43 'Warship' where it would be replaced by one of the SR's all-electric Class 71 locomotives. All-green No E5003 passes Goring-by-Sea in West Sussex on 11 November that year with a wonderful goods train, and one of a decent length for southern England. *Author*

▼ There seems to be few pictures in circulation featuring Bulleid's curious 1941-built Class 72 C-C all-electric locomotives with full yellow ends working non-passenger services. However, shortly before withdrawal in 1969 the first of a class of three locomotives, No 20001, was photographed at Burgess Hill station on the Brighton main line with an up van train for London Bridge. Forty-three years after the event these machines look almost archaic. *Author*

▲ A significant clue to identifying a newspaper train (especially a long-distance working), as distinct from a parcels/postal working, was to search the consist for a single passenger coach amongst the vans. After sorting and bundling papers on the train the staff would usually retire to such a vehicle for the remainder of the outward journey and for the whole of the return, thereby 'getting their heads down' for a few hours. Class 73 electro-diesel No E6040 (later No 73113) in blue livery but with small yellow warning panel, is seen heading such a train as it leaves Worthing Central on the Coastway line in August 1967 with the returning Chichester to Bricklayers Arms empties. *Author*

▼ More early-style container wagons as well as some general goods are on the move at Eastleigh as this Class 33/0 in green livery but with small yellow warning panel, rushes through the station in the down direction during 1966. The line was electrified the following year, the lineside hut was flattened, the semaphores removed, the signalbox closed and the up island platform abandoned. The distant all-green light 'Crompton' and the old DEMU are now also history, but the author is still 'hanging on in there'! *Author*

▲ The official British Railways caption on this Western Region publicity shot states 'Diesel loco *Lion* (experimental engine) on the 1.30pm Paddington to Plymouth parcels at Twyford, 2 July 1962 – negative No C38347'. The information is not inaccurate, but perhaps No D0260 is deserving of a better description. The one-off locomotive was produced in May 1962 through a collaboration between Birmingham Railway Carriage & Wagon Company, Sulzer Brothers and Associated Electrical Industries plus subsidiaries such as British Thomson-Houston. The 2,750hp machine travelled only 80,000 miles in its short life because it suffered from electrical problems, including several generator flashovers, a control cubicle fire and serious oil losses from its diesel engine, notwithstanding the collapse of the BRCW company. *BR(WR)*

▼ Cheating slightly on the 'goods and freight' description is this interesting night shot of the original prototype *Deltic* DP1. The locomotive is seen in nocturnal pose at what is thought to be Glasgow Central station with a 'Canadian Trade Mission' special exhibition train with a non-passenger BG van leading. Unlike any other class of diesel locomotive the production 'Deltics' were exclusively express passenger locomotives and appearances on goods or freight workings were rare and regarded as newsworthy by railway magazines of the era. Ironically, in 2011 a preserved 'Deltic' was hired for commercial freight haulage in the Lynemouth/North Blyth area, eventually reaching Fort William! *GEC Traction Limited*

1950s AND 1960s IN COLOUR

▲ 'Britannia' class 4-6-2 No 70029 once rejoiced in carrying the name *Shooting Star*, but as was common towards the end of the steam era many nameplates were removed, some by persons unknown. Heading north from Skipton and building up steam pressure as it drifts down the 1 in 214 towards Hellifield the BR Standard Pacific will soon be working hard on the long 15-mile drag up to Blea Moor on the Settle and Carlisle line. The mixed freight is the 12.55 Leeds Stourton to Carlisle. *Gavin Morrison*

▶ One hopes that the no doubt significant noise made by BR Standard 9F class 2-10-0 No 92138 did not terrify the poor beasts visible in the leading livestock wagons coupled next to the locomotive. On 24 August 1963, a lengthy down fitted freight comprising elderly four-wheeled vacuum-braked wagons comes off the line from Oxford and Evesham at Norton Junction and heads for Worcester. The lines to the right head south towards Cheltenham and Gloucester. *Michael Mensing*

▲ If ever a standard class of freight engine earned its keep while handsomely repaying initial capital investment costs, it was the LMSR Stanier 8F 2-8-0s. Some 852 examples were built at over a dozen locations between 1935 and 1946, many during the Second World War. A large number of 8Fs saw service overseas including, inter alia, Iran, Iraq, Israel, Egypt and Turkey. Of the 666 examples eventually owned by BR only a handful have been preserved, although some have been repatriated from Turkey. Here, No 48430 heads an up coal train through Acocks Green & South Yardley station on the GWR Birmingham to Leamington route, on 26 September 1963. *Michael Mensing*

◄ The lower quadrant semaphore signals give a strong indication that this scene was captured on a former GWR route. Clanking its way past Hollinswood a few miles east of Wellington, Salop, on 27 August 1962, ex-LMSR 8F 2-8-0 No 48478 heads an up goods bound for the Wolverhampton area. A nearby line from Hollinswood Goods sidings to Stirchley had closed in February 1959. *Michael Mensing*

► This view shows the interesting track configuration at Aynho Junction a few miles south of Banbury. Coming off the Oxford line with a northbound freight on 29 August 1962 is 'Black Five' No 44775, the locomotive being clean enough to detect its pleasant lined-black livery. The track on the right is the down road of the 'Birmingham Direct' route via High Wycombe, now associated with Chiltern Trains.
Michael Mensing

▼ Rounding off a wonderful quartet of LMS locomotive-hauled freights is this express northbound fitted freight seen hammering through Droitwich Road (Goods) on the direct Ashchurch to Bromsgrove route behind three-cylinder 'Jubilee' class 4-6-0 No 45712 *Victory* at 6.51pm on 3 May 1963, bathed in low, warm evening lighting. The train would soon be tackling the formidable Lickey incline, but would a banker be required? *Michael Mensing*

▲ The GWR's version of the LMS 8F, although of much earlier design, was the 2800/2884 class of 8F power 2-8-0s. Originally introduced by Churchward in 1903 it says much for the basic design that a batch of similar Collett locomotives appeared in 1938 with only detail differences. In this delightful scene dating back to 16 May 1964, Collett No 3809 plods out of Ledbury Tunnel, between Hereford and Worcester, with a load that largely comprises coal from South Wales. The train is banked by 2-6-2T No 4124, the crew no doubt inhaling some of the freight engine's exhaust. *Michael Mensing*

▼ The year before this photograph was taken, on 12 October 1963, BR had lost a staggering £102 million, which is over £2 billion in 2012 values. This made the Beeching review all the more important as there was a perceived urgent need to reduce the loss and therefore the taxpayer subsidy to the railways. 'Modified Hall' 4-6-0 No 7901 *Dodington Hall* makes its way along the old Great Central Railway link between Banbury and Woodford Halse; closing this line eventually saved money. The northbound freight makes a wonderful sight as it passes within a mile or so of Thorpe Mandeville village. *Michael Mensing*

▶ Lined-green livery with brass adornments are associated by many with the products of Swindon. Certainly the aesthetic appeal of 'Hall' class No 4998 *Eyton Hall* is obvious as it passes Madeley Junction near Wellington, Salop, with an eastbound goods on 27 August 1962. The line to the left heads towards Ironbridge and is still used for power station coal trains, although this junction signalbox has long since disappeared.
Michael Mensing

▶ By 1961, the total receipts from BR's nationwide freight traffic were £255.6 million, excluding parcels and mail sources, but direct costs were £268.5 million and when indirect costs and overheads were added the total spiralled to £331.6 million, resulting in an annual loss of £76 million (over £1.5 billion in current values!). Possibly making a small profit is 5700 class 0-6-0PT No 9639 seen leaving the Madeley Junction loop with down loaded coal wagons. *Michael Mensing*

◀ The Beeching 'Reshaping Report' delivered some quite dramatic statistics. For example, one-third of BR's entire track mileage carried only one per cent of total freight traffic and half of all route mileage, 8,900 miles, carried only five per cent of total freight ton miles. Most of the freight carried was also of the 'wrong' type, being of the hugely loss-making wagonload variety. In the latter category is this up freight on 26 September 1960, headed by LMS 4F 0-6-0 No 44386 and seen between the North and Middle Harecastle Tunnels, north-west of Stoke-on-Trent. *Michael Mensing*

▼ Trains have not passed through this delightful landscape for more than 45 years. The sparsely populated route from Dumfries to Stranraer (Challoch Junction) was a prime candidate for closure and it duly succumbed in mid-1965. Heading east with an up freight is 'Crab' 2-6-0 No 42919 on 13 July 1963, seen crossing Urr Viaduct near Dalbeattie, between Castle Douglas and Dumfries, on the old Glasgow & South Western Railway route. There were no 100-tonne bogie wagons around in those days and the little four-wheelers look truly diminutive. *Michael Mensing*

▲ It may now seem hard to believe but in many ways this action shot shows a steam-era freightliner train because there are a large number of containers on board, all part of BR's 'Door to Door' service. As early as 1949 BR was running advertisements under their 'Get Things Moving' marketing campaign. The full quote was 'Use British Railways' specialised Road/Rail container service. Containers give a door to door delivery, with a minimum of packing and handling. There are 20,000 wagons many of them covered types and completely waterproof – ideal for conveyance of a wide range of commodities.' 'Jubilee' class No 45675 *Hardy* thrashes along under the overhead wires of the Morecambe to Lancaster electrified line at Scale Hall, Lancaster, in 1965 with a Heysham to Leeds freight. The locomotive was withdrawn in June 1967. *Gavin Morrison*

▼ An all-out effort is made by Class 5MT No 45455 of Carlisle Kingmoor shed on 4 February 1967 as it makes slow progress some two miles distant from the infamous Shap Summit. The freight had taken about two hours to travel the 30 miles from Carlisle to Strickland, having been looped on more than one occasion. Again, 'Door to Door' containers are to the fore. The 'Black Five' is fitted with a small snowplough and the lamp headcode signifies 'express freight, livestock or ballast train NOT fitted with continuous brake'. *Gavin Morrison*

▲ The photographer has always been meticulous in recording locomotive numbers but this O4 class 2-8-0 of GCR origin was so filthy that only the numbers 638xx could be made out. Heading a down coal train the locomotive is depicted south of Heath station on the long-closed Great Central Railway line near Chesterfield on 29 September 1959. Out of the 145.7 million tons of coal carried by BR each year in 1959 27.6 million tons, or 19 per cent, was for the domestic market. At this time demand for coal was rapidly diminishing, removing any opportunity for growth in market share. *Michael Mensing*

▼ During the mid-1960s a general malaise swept through the various depots and amongst the footplate staff on all regions of BR, resulting in filthy and grimy machinery running on all regions throughout the national network. SR U class 2-6-0 No 31632 of Maunsell design and 1928 build was no exception to the rule as it rolled into Yeovil Junction with a down freight on 17 September 1964. Three ESSO fuel tankers have been included in a fairly light load. The headlamp code, single lamp, bottom right as viewed, signifies a 'branch freight train'. *Gavin Morrison*

▲ While this down freight may not be comprised of many wagons it is obvious that this loaded mineral train is heavy enough to require banking assistance on the climb to Beattock Summit, just over four miles from Beattock station. 'Black Five' No 45490 is making every effort and at the rear of the train, Fairburn 2-6-4T No 42127 provides a welcome push, seen on 4 July 1964. The scene is dated by the road vehicles. *Michael Mensing*

▼ From 5 June 1950 new train identity lamp codes were introduced. The positions of the front end (or tender) lamp irons allowed for many permutations and this configuration of a bottom centre and (as viewed) left-hand lamp was described thus: 'parcels, fish, fruit, horse, livestock, meat, milk, pigeon or perishables train composed entirely of vehicles conforming to coaching stock requirements. Express freight, livestock, perishables, or ballast train piped fitted throughout with the automatic vacuum brake operative on not less than half the vehicles.' Certainly, No 92228 looks in a hurry with a down fitted freight at Lapworth water troughs on 12 July 1966. Note the large water tank and the water in the troughs in the centre of both track alignments. *Michael Mensing*

◄ This photograph is extremely rare in that it shows the only example of the Metropolitan-Vickers Class 28 Co-Bo fleet that appeared in BR corporate blue. The class of 20 locomotives employed 1,200hp Crossley two-stroke diesel engines that proved problematical and all locomotives were withdrawn between December 1967 and September 1968. Seen near Grange-over-Sands on 21 June 1968, No D5701 is heading the Whitehaven to Heysham Moss tanks. *Michael Mensing*

◄ Once the Class 17 'Clayton' diesels proved to be unreliable and fell out of operational favour they were exiled to the remote parts of the BR network. It was a national scandal that 117 of the 900hp centre-cab machines were ordered, many before the design was tried and tested. Two 450hp Paxman engines were employed but they proved troublesome. The last of the class was delivered in April 1965 and by December 1971 all had been withdrawn! One of the areas where the class could latterly be found at work was the Cumbrian coast and here, Nos D8506 and D8500 approach Workington station with a southbound freight on 20 June 1968. *Michael Mensing*

◄ While the operating authorities opted for an insurance policy of working two Class 17 'Clayton' locomotives in multiple this little BR/Sulzer Type 2, No D5197 (later Class 25 No 25047), was entrusted with this up fitted freight, seen approaching Harbury Tunnel, south-east of Leamington, on 27 September 1965. However, in this case it may have been the slightly higher horsepower rating that ensured the motive power was deemed to be fit for purpose. The filthy green livery is hardly a ringing endorsement for its home depot. *Michael Mensing*

▶ The headcode on this diesel-hauled train signifies an 'express freight, livestock, perishables, or ballast train partly fitted with NOT less than one third of the vacuum braked vehicles connected by vacuum pipe to the engine or express freight with a limited load of vehicles NOT fitted with continuous brake'. North British MAN-engined Class 21 (as it was to become) No D6124 is seen in evening sunshine just north of Kinnaber Junction, Montrose, with a down freight in July 1964. The locomotive was later re-engined and rated at 1,350hp, becoming a Class 29. It had a total working life of just 12 years. There seems to be at least half a dozen brake vans in the consist! *Michael Mensing*

▶ The English Electric 1,750hp diesel-electric Co-Cos were arguably the most successful British freight locomotives of the era with the optimum combination of middle power range, good route availability, and a reasonable weight for braking purposes, but above all else great reliability. Westbound near Ancaster in Lincolnshire is No D6745 (later 37045) on 28 May 1966 with a long rake of coal empties comprising train 7M69. Such wagons would soon become redundant as air braking gradually made inroads into BR's freight rolling stock. *Michael Mensing*

▶ Passing delightful scenery at Loch Treig on the West Highland line while making its way to Fort William is English Electric 1,000hp Type 1 No D8095 (later Class 20 No 20095) on 16 July 1965, the time of year and the northern latitude easily allowing action photography at 7.05pm. The mixed line of wagons was a reminder that such loads combined with terminal expenses, marshalling, trip working, the provision of wagons for small loads, paper documentation and road collection and delivery were all costly and seriously dented the potential profitability of goods and freight workings. *Michael Mensing*

▲ Slowly but surely the arrival of new diesel locomotives in accordance with the Modernisation Plan made inroads to the ranks of steam engines. In broad brush terms one diesel could replace three steam locomotives such was their high availability, with in many cases the diesels being ready for use at little more than the touch of a button. Loading dusty coal, lubrication with messy oil cans and choking on ash deposits were becoming things of the past, with some express passenger train drivers even wearing white coats and jackets. BRCW/Sulzer 1,550hp Type 3 No D6508 is seen passing Norton Halt near Worcester with empty tankers returning to Fawley via Oxford on 24 August 1963. The little station closed in January 1966. *Michael Mensing*

▼ This 'Crompton', No D6549, has yet to become Class 33 No 33031 as it sweeps into Southampton Central station with ESSO fuel tank wagons from Fawley on 12 September 1965. The locomotive is in attractive all-green livery and is obviously better cared for than the above member of the class. These purposeful all-rounders could be seen in the area for another 30 years and although they travelled widely in the autumn of their lives they were always associated with the Southern Region. This particular locomotive was withdrawn due to fire damage incurred at Tonbridge in the late 1980s. *Gavin Morrison*

▲ In original condition, this Haymarket English Electric Type 4, No D266, heads a very mixed parcels train past Drem, to the east of Edinburgh in 1961. The branch line to the left terminates at North Berwick, which in common with the East Coast Main Line, was eventually electrified. The locomotive, later No 40066, spent its entire 21-year working life, from 1960 to 1981, at Haymarket depot to the west of the Scottish capital, although it was finally cut up at Swindon in October 1981. *Gavin Morrison*

▼ Train 8M59 has left the marshalling yard at Healey Mills and is seen making its way past Heaton Lodge Junction to the west of Mirfield on 14 May 1974. In charge on this day was green Class 40, with full yellow cab front, No 40183, one of the few then remaining in this livery. The train will later cross the Pennines into Lancashire. The mixed status of the load is remarkable, with steel bars, minerals, coal and even an army tank visible. *Gavin Morrison*

▲ The Brush/Sulzer Type 4s, later Class 47s, were to become truly ubiquitous with 512 examples being built, which at various times could be seen working throughout the BR network. On a sunny 29 September 1973 No D1804 (later No 47323) looks good in its two-tone green paintwork as it speeds south through Harbury cutting with a car-carrying hot-shot, 4V37. The Ford motor company has used the railways to transport cars and parts for many years and this train seems to be conveying mostly Ford Escorts built at Halewood, from Garston to a distribution terminal at Dagenham. *Gavin Morrison*

▼ One of the serious problems in making coal trains profitable was the vast multiplicity of destinations. There were over 600 rail-connected pits at the time of Nationalisation leading to immense complexity of movement, especially when different types and quality of coal were added to the equation. Although 57 million tons of coal were moved by block train, a massive 89 million tons were moved by the complex staging of wagons, a process that cost twice as much per ton delivered. One of the heavy 1Co-Co1 2,500hp BR/Brush Type 4 'Peaks', No D154 (later No 46017) in green livery, is seen between Duffield and Derby on 30 April 1966 with a long Class 8 coal haul. *Michael Mensing*

▲ A sheer delight for all Class 40 fans is this impression of No D316 sweeping through Queensville Curve at Stafford on 6 October 1962 with a down parcels train, initially bound for Crewe. At this time folding headcode discs were used in the same way as oil lamps on steam locomotives to denote the train classification, this working being pipe-fitted throughout with automatic vacuum-brake operative on not less than half the vehicles. The locomotive is in original condition without being corrupted by yellow warning panels of any description. *Michael Mensing*

▶ This photograph depicts Brush Type 2 No D5549, also in original condition, when it was still fitted with a 1,250hp Mirrlees diesel engine and in green livery with body stripes, but without visibility embellishments. It would later become No 31131 and be fitted with a 1,470hp English Electric prime mover. The up fitted freight is seen to the east of Chelmsford at 11.58am on 8 June 1962. *Michael Mensing*

▲ Summer flowers encrust the embankment near the River Bervie Viaduct, south of Drumlithe, on the Montrose to Stonehaven route as BRCW/Sulzer Type 2 No D5306 (later Class 26 No 26006) runs deeper into Scotland with a down fitted freight heading in the Aberdeen direction, on 15 July 1964. These gruff-sounding 1,160hp six-cylinder machines were latterly associated with Scotland until their final demise. Built from 1958 the machines were well thought of for their size and although withdrawals started in 1977 it was 1993 before the last was withdrawn, a remarkable lifespan of 35 years and considerably outliving their Class 27 cousins. *Michael Mensing*

▼ Although taken over 40 years ago this is a historically significant image, not only because it shows an early example of a modern container on an air-braked Freightliner train, or Carlisle station before it was disfigured with overhead wires, but because it shows elite Class 50s (the last diesel-engined 'passenger' locomotive built in the UK for BR) working both freight and passenger trains. On 28 June 1968, No D427 (later No 50027 *Lion*) enters the station from Glasgow while in the right background, No D413 (later No 50013 *Agincourt*) heads 1S57, the down 'Royal Scot' from London Euston. To many this scene will be as nostalgic as viewing steam over Shap. *Michael Mensing*

British Railways to British Rail

After the publication of BRB's *The Reshaping of British Railways* report there was a predictable fall out of sentiment where few people wanted railway lines or goods depots to close, but nobody was prepared to stump up the cash to underwrite the massive losses being incurred by the railways. These continued to be met by the government, in other words the taxpayer at large. Although we are not concerned here with passenger train services, following the publication of the report there had been various marketing initiatives to try to convey a modern image to the travelling public. Such public relations exercises as 'XP64', the introduction of the novel BR 'double-arrow' logo, and much later the successful advent of 'InterCity' were all positive steps along the way as slowly but surely the railways modernised.

On the goods and freight side progress was also steady but slow. There was a certain irony in that while minor depots, goods yards and branch and minor lines closed, theoretically saving BR shedloads of money, the withdrawal of facilities reduced total freight tonnage and therefore gross income. By the end of 1968 steam traction had disappeared and large numbers of small low-powered diesel locomotives had also been prematurely withdrawn from service. Of the more successful early classes much of the fleet was gradually fitted with a train air-braking facility, although a few vacuum-braked examples continued in service until the 1980s.

From the mid-1970s, new-build locomotives were air-braked only, reflecting the radical changes that had occurred in the BR wagon fleet. This change was commensurate with the Beeching recommendations for new modern wagons that did not have to be compatible with what then existed. Between 1969 and 1980 air-braked wagons grew from a few hundred to 14 per cent, or 1 in 7 of the entire fleet, whereas vacuum-braked examples hovered around the 40 per cent mark. This still left a sizeable number of unbraked or manually braked wagons, which were the obvious targets for early withdrawal.

There were of course hundreds of different types of wagon built to accommodate a wide range of goods and materials. This caused operational problems due mainly to different braking systems, resulting in the inability to provide fully fitted freight trains. It was theoretically possible to have a wagon consist with an incompatible mixture of air-braked, vacuum-braked and manually braked vehicles. While in the main, freight trains were formed of either vacuum-braked or air-braked wagons there were some curios. For example, in Cornwall old wooden-bodied vacuum-braked china clay wagons would occasionally be mixed with modern air-braked vehicles, which were normally positioned next to the locomotives. These modern wagons had a 'through vacuum pipe' that allowed the locomotive train brake to be used on the trailing older type of vacuum-braked wagons.

Where freights were unfitted a brake or 'guard's' van was normally attached, although the sight of a brake van did not necessarily mean that a goods train was unfitted. For example, brake vans were used when an element of propelling was the norm. Once brake vans were no longer used travelling train guards and shunters had to be accommodated in the rear cab of the locomotive.

Although elementary it should perhaps be explained that the reason for a preoccupation with braking systems and goods wagon braking compatibility, is calculating the total braking power of any particular train, which is an overriding and all-important safety factor. Every locomotive has its own brake force rating but the amount of train braking available has a direct effect on total train weight and train speed. The maximum weight of a fully fitted train is considerably higher than that of an unfitted, partially fitted or 'loose coupled' train in comparable conditions. In the case of the latter only the locomotive and to a much lesser extent the brake van have the braking power to stop a train of a given tonnage within a certain distance at a certain speed.

In many areas with steep inclines unfitted trains had to stop to enable individual wagons with primitive manual braking systems to have their brakes 'pinned down' or 'picked up' at relevant locations before proceeding. Particularly in the early days of dieselisation but continuing well into the 1970s, locomotives were often attached to 'brake tenders', which were heavily ballasted normally vacuum-braked vehicles attached either immediately in front of or behind the train locomotive(s) to improve the total available brake force (see illustrations).

If factors such as maximum load, maximum line speed, braking systems, loading systems and coupling compatibility are all taken into consideration it soon becomes apparent how complex running a simple mixed goods or freight train could be. In terms of couplings certain wagons could not be operated on the 'hump yard' method of wagon marshalling. Also, mixed trains obviously had to run at the speed of the slowest permitted speed of any one vehicle within the consist.

In addition to changes in braking systems the other major development in terms of wagons during the 1970s and 1980s were overall increases in their size and therefore payload, a greater use of bogie wagons where appropriate, and a very significant increase in the number of private-owner wagons working on BR rails. By 1980, there were 18,000 private-owner wagons and of these about two-thirds were petroleum tankers. Although not universal there was an increase in permitted running speed for freights as wagon wheelbases became longer and roller bearings and disc brakes made an appearance. An increase in axle loading to 22.5 tonnes on some routes resulted in wagons of 45-tonnes gross laden weight being delivered and, soon, 90-tonne bogie wagons appeared, their weight obviously being carried on four axles.

There were some outstanding success stories during this period particularly the 'merry-go-round' (mgr) pit-to-power station coal train operation, the significant developments in handling stone and aggregate traffic from the Somerset quarries, and the remarkable development of the freightliner trains and containerisation. The combination of new wagons, new locomotives and new infrastructure all working bulk freight in block loads was exactly what the Beeching Reshaping Report envisaged, using the benefits that the railways offered to the full and making a contribution to the elusive operating profit for what had then become British Rail.

Commensurate with this increase in mgr and stone traffic the Chief Civil Engineer again relaxed axle loadings on some routes to 25 tonnes and this resulted in 50-tonne gross loaded weight hopper wagons appearing. In time this would also have an effect as 100-tonne bogie wagons appeared.

One of the major problems with BR's entire wagon, carriage and locomotive movements system was the lack of a modern approach to the subject and the absence of real time data in what was rapidly becoming a computerised world. As already mentioned, trying to track the progress of a wagon was extremely difficult, especially where the vehicle had to be marshalled and shunted a number of times and perhaps travelling in the consist of three successive trains to complete various stages of its journey. On occasions wagons were 'lost' with much derision coming from the customer when this occurred.

It is now hard to imagine several hundreds of thousands of tickets and dockets hanging on clips in goods offices the length and breadth of the country, although to be fair, Telex (a bit like telegrams) machines were also used. In 1971, approval for the purchase and development of a Total Operations Processing System, popularly known as 'TOPS', was given. This system would provide planning, operating and maintenance departments with up to date and accurate data relating to all aspects of the freight business. TOPS would identify the precise location of every wagon (and eventually locomotives and carriages) to improve the overall efficiency of freight wagon movement and usage, and give both railway employees and customers current information about any consignment, in turn, keeping their customers up to date.

Wagon utilisation statistics were awful and once a wagon had left its original loading point little further information was available until it reached its destination. If a wagon did not arrive as scheduled its 'path' would have to be traced and a single shunting or wagon identification error could find a wagon at the back end of a vast marshalling yard. Unusually for BR in the 1970s, they did not try to create a brand-new and previously untested system. TOPS had been tried and tested by 'espee', the Southern Pacific Railroad company in the western USA. A main frame computer was located in London and fortunately BR had recently upgraded its telecommunications system, enabling access to the TOPS computer from depots and offices nationwide.

A stack of real-time data suddenly became available regarding the movement and position of individual wagons, consignments, the arrival and departure times of wagons and complete trains. Locomotives were brought into the system with overall full implementation taking four years. There were some amusing stories along the way such as a number of wagons having different serial numbers on each side, wagon numbers being duplicated and BR having more wagons than its census suggested!

Overall, TOPS soon proved to be a great bonus to the operators informing them of how many trains there were at any location, the train weight and the number of wagons in the train. They also knew the number of wagons in a marshalling yard, goods yard or customer siding (each was given a unique identity code number), whether the wagon was empty or loaded, its weight and brake force, whether it was running to time, or not, where empty wagons of a certain type were located (to meet an instant customer demand) and, if loaded, when they would become available. There was also an important historical record of recent movements, all used to measure efficiency, loads, utilisation and mileages for maintenance purposes.

In developing mgr, aggregate and other increasing types of traffic the appallingly slow turn-round times that had been identified in earlier years was radically improved. In the case of mgr trains the wagons were stationary only on the weekends and rarely were they used as coal bunkers, so vividly described in the Reshaping Report. Within the mgr operation wagons were loaded and unloaded while on the move and special slow-speed control equipment was eventually fitted to the locomotives working such diagrams. The speed control system was calibrated in notches with each notch representing an increase or decrease in speed of one-half a mile per hour.

The HAA-style wagons (and associated subclasses) were top loaded via conveyor belt, silo and chute, while under frame hopper discharge was employed. No marshalling was involved and at both loading and unloading points trains mostly ran in a continuous loop. These trains normally loaded at between 32 and 40 wagons, each with a gross loaded weight of 50 tonnes. Formations were fixed although, for various reasons, some circuit formations were shorter or, less frequently, longer than the norm.

These developments could never have been achieved without a tri-partied effort involving BR, the National Coal Board and the Central Electricity Generating Board. From the mid-1960s to the mid-1970s there were massive infrastructure improvements to accommodate the new mgr trains. Gone were the days of multiple sidings full of coal loads and empties all waiting for the next piece of paper to be delivered to the goods office authorising movement. The clanking of couplings and the squeal of wheel flanges disappeared as shunting locomotives were dispensed with and the gliding of roller bearings on welded rail produced a new silence on the railways.

The new system lent itself to supply and demand and at the touch of an input button coal could be directed to wherever it was needed. It was not only power stations that were fitted-out for an mgr style of operation but also many cement works and steel works sites. Over a period of 18 years, between 1965 and 1983, over 11,000 HAA-style four-wheeled air-braked hopper wagons entered service. As an aside it seemed strange to be on Shap Summit during 2010 to witness what was then the last train to be formed entirely of HAA hoppers, 6F51 the 08.01 Earle's Sidings to New Cumnock, via Carlisle. Modern high-capacity bogie wagons had gradually displaced HAA mgr types from the early days of privatisation.

The stone and aggregate business also benefited from modernisation. In the late 1960s there continued to be a boom in motorway construction and other major area redevelopments. Quarries nationwide responded to meet demand and in Somerset both Foster Yeoman (now Aggregate Industries) and Amalgamated Roadstone Corporation (now Hanson Aggregates) spent considerable sums of money developing Merehead and Whatley Quarries.

Merehead churned out some 2,000 tons of stone per hour with annual production topping 5 million tonnes by 1970. Other aggregate companies also got in on the act including English China Clays, Bardon and a number of others who focussed on Mountsorrel in Leicestershire and also, by way of example, the Peak Forest/Great Rocks/Buxton areas of the Derbyshire Peak District.

In the south-east a large number of unloading sites doubling as distribution centres spawned. Between 1969 and 1974 the rail stone/aggregates business grew from 2 to 10 million tons per annum, putting a smile on the face of BR as a much-needed freight success story unfolded. During the 1980s some 5 million tons of railborne stone and aggregates were hauled out of just the Somerset hills. Generally this sector of the freight business prospered, eventually leading to the operation of 'jumbo' stone trains between Merehead and Acton, where multi-terminal train splits were made. Gradually a high percentage of four-wheeled wagons were replaced by ultra-modern high-capacity bogie wagons.

On the downside the whole massive operation of BR freight train haulage in the period covered by this chapter was the ageing BR motive power that was really not up to the task. Nearly all of the old Pilot Scheme locomotives, including an amazing array of totally unsuccessful classes, and a myriad of prototypes and pioneers, had gone by the early 1970s, and by 1977 all the main line diesel-hydraulic classes, mainly associated with the Western Region, had been withdrawn. Pairs of Class 20s, 25s, 26s, 31s, 33s and 37s were commonplace, supported by ageing Class 40s, 46s and 47s, and they fulfilled the primary freight requirement, but only at the expense of reliability and therefore availability.

Occasionally, passenger locomotives were employed on freight traffic, such as Class 45s and 50s, but new-generation high-powered machinery was urgently required. This miscellany of surviving classes had, on the whole, done a good

▶ After passenger services were withdrawn between Carmarthen and Aberystwyth in remote West Wales, it was a patient photographer who attempted to record the ever-decreasing branch goods trains that continued to erratically run between Carmarthen and Newcastle Emlyn, and Carmarthen and Lampeter via Pencader (with trips to Felin Fach and Pont Llanio for milk tanks). In April 1970, 1,700hp 'Hymek' Class 35 No D7070 from the Beyer Peacock factory passes the hamlet of Dolgran near Pencader with just four coal wagons for Newcastle Emlyn, precisely the type of train that the 1963 Reshaping Report said should be eradicated. *Author*

job for BR with Classes 20, 33 and 37 in particular having had an excellent availability rating, all things considered. There had been a massive underinvestment in dedicated freight motive power and in the early 1970s most of the locomotives employed were already (at least) between 10 and 15 years old. A new freight locomotive was desperately needed whereby old locomotives could be retired and costly double heading could be eliminated. The new-build was eventually dubbed Class 56, which was seen as the motive power panacea to bulk block train haulage problems, including the aggregate traffic mentioned above.

BR issued a specification within their tender that called for an air-braked locomotive in the Type 5 category with a rating of more than 3,000hp. The locomotives were to have diesel-electric traction, ac electrical power and electronic control systems using an alternator. Maximum speed was set at 80mph with a 21-tonne axle load based on Co-Co bogies. The first 30 locomotives fitted with Ruston Paxman 16-cylinder 3,250hp engines and Brush-built major electrical machines of a UK specification, were built in Romania, where an immediate start could be made on construction. Subsequent locomotives were built at BREL workshops at Doncaster and Crewe. The first example appeared in August 1976 but it would be the end of February 1977 before it was accepted into BR service. The last of the 135-strong fleet was completed at Crewe in September 1984. Unfortunately, the class proved to be troublesome and this initial unreliability did their reputation no good at all, especially with certain customers, including Foster Yeoman. During 1980 BR conducted trials on heavy Somerset stone trains using pairs of Class 50 express passenger locomotives. By the early 1980s frustrations with BR must have been at an all-time high when Foster Yeoman decided to procure its own locomotives to haul its own wagons.

The full story of this remarkable innovation could fill a book in its own right; suffice to say here, that in cooperation with General Motors in North America a novel solution to an age-old problem was solved: to produce a technologically advanced, high-powered, reliable, tried-and-tested, fit for purpose locomotive to the UK loading gauge, on time and in budget. There was the usual ballyhoo regarding acceptance trials and the expected trade union opposition to anything new, unless financial sweeteners were in the offing, but in retrospect the entire operation was successful. In the long term, well into the 21st century, the initiative would impact freight operations throughout the UK and Europe as the benefits of North American motive power procurements were universally embraced.

Hot on the heels of the Class 56 was the Class 58, a fairly cheap and cheerful but functional locomotive with a simple modular construction affording easy access for maintenance purposes. It was not possible for the train crew to walk from cab to cab as only side access panels were provided. Again, primary electrical machines were by Brush and, again, Ruston Paxman provided the prime mover but this time the 12-cylinder RK3ACT 3,300hp diesel engine. It was marginally heavier and longer than the Class 56. The primary role of the Class 58s was to haul mgr colliery-to-power station coal trains and in 1989 the entire fleet of 50 locomotives was allocated to the 'Freight (Power Station Coal) Yorkshire Class 58 Pool' based at Toton. Their availability figures were not as high as anticipated but for between 14 and 18 years the locomotives worked hard on the coal train circuit. In their later years they performed other duties, including some on the Southern Region. The entire class was simply switched off in September 2001 having become victims of new procurements by the English Welsh & Scottish company following the privatisation of BR.

The last gasp for the British freight diesel locomotive industry was to be the Class 60. It is distinctly possible that after 165 years of locomotive building in the UK that the Brush Class 60 will be the last class of main line

◀ Although these hopper wagons passing West Worthing in June 1982 are four-wheelers this is a complete air-braked 'block' train working, which was the sign of things to come. The age of the air brake had truly arrived, far fewer goods and freight trains on BR were vacuum braked and the guards or brake van was becoming redundant. With a few lingering exceptions, such as departmental trains and pockets of special cases such as local china clay wagons in Cornwall, technology was rapidly changing. No 47086 *Colossus* is seen heading the Ardingly to Westbury and Whatley Quarry roadstone empties. The three-road carriage shed on the left has since been demolished. *Author*

diesel locomotive constructed in these islands. No doubt envious of the North American Class 59 procurement by Foster Yeoman, BR tabled the issue of long-term freight locomotive requirements. All of the old classes from the 1950s and 1960s were getting long in the tooth and to compound the problem they realised that the Class 56s and to a lesser extent the Class 58s were not all that they were cracked up to be.

In 1987, BR issued tenders for the construction of 100 3,000hp+ locomotives with a high technical specification and electronic control systems featuring microprocessors as well as a multiple working capability and air brakes. The order was won by Brush in May 1988 and a contract awarded. It was claimed that maintenance costs of the new locomotive would be one-third that of Classes 56 and 58. An obvious part of the specification was for a slow-speed control system. The frame was to be of advanced monocoque construction. Having opted for 16 cylinders in the Class 56, 12 cylinders in the Class 58, the Class 60 had an eight-cylinder Blackstone 8MB275T diesel engine rated at 3,100hp, which powered Brush main electrical machines.

The locomotives were to be built at Loughborough but with the bodies constructed by Procor. Unfortunately, the project was rushed and the timescales signed up were too tight to allow full testing. The first locomotive was delivered in June 1989 and on schedule. However, several problems emerged almost immediately, especially with control software and suspension parts. So many modifications were required that there was a queue at the Brush works for locomotives awaiting rectification and over a year elapsed before the first of the 100 ordered Class 60s was accepted by BR. By this time there is little doubt that BR was wishing that they too had bought American.

Even when all of the bugs had been ironed out the class failed to deliver either the availability figures or the anticipated fuel consumption savings originally promised. The Class 60s were geared so that they could run at a maximum of 60mph but had a greater haulage capability at low speeds and consequently they could haul very heavy loads, hence their nickname of 'Tugs'. Although following privatisation and particularly following the procurement of 250 Class 66s from North America, large numbers of the class were withdrawn and placed in store, but with many of the new General Motors locomotives subsequently transferred to Europe, it was announced in 2011 that up to 20 Class 60s would be refurbished and labelled 'Super Sixties', giving them a life extension of a further decade. On reflection and bearing in mind BR's remarkable freight train history, it is good to know that a handful of British-built diesel locomotives will enjoy something of an Indian summer.

Meanwhile, another British locomotive procurement that did absolutely nothing for the reputation of BR or Brush, or for that matter British engineering, was the case of the Class 92 dual-voltage locomotive. This was later described by the managing director of RfD as 'the most complicated locomotive known to mankind'. Channel Tunnel freight traffic estimates were for 35 trains per day each way by the end of the 1990s. These estimates proved to be hopelessly optimistic. For this traffic the purchase of 30 Class 92 locomotives had been authorised, in addition to 750 new-build wagons, 450 for intermodal use and 300 for the automotive industry.

At 5,360–6,760hp the new locomotives would be extremely powerful and designed to haul heavy trains from France via the tunnel to the north of England and Scotland. A further seven locomotives were ordered for EPS (European Passenger Services) and nine for SNCF (Société Nationale Chemins de Fer [French Railways]). The first shock was that the 1990 cost of £102 million had escalated to £120 million by 1992. The next problem was delayed delivery with RfD having the prospect of having no locomotives to haul their trains through the Channel Tunnel on the opening day. At one point, BR was considering withdrawing completely from Channel Tunnel freight!

In a continuing exercise in 'how not to do it', when the locomotives were finally delivered in 1994/95 they were found to interfere with Railtrack's domestic track circuiting and signalling. They could be used in the tunnel but nowhere else. In fact, it was June 1996 before Class 92s could work between the tunnel and Wembley. In an appalling case of technical incompetence, or at least a lack of foresight, the locomotives were not cleared to work on the West Coast Main Line until 1998. The first through freight train negotiated the tunnel in June 1994 but traffic was so disappointing that BR had to set aside £500 million to write off freight assets to meet the costs of minimum usage charges payable to Eurotunnel.

Operationally, the Class 92 eventually delivered in accordance with original performance levels and most of the fleet are in everyday use today, but for the first four years of their existence they were a technical disaster due to external influences. Although not for this book, there was another colossal howler when in 1995 a dozen Class 37 locomotives were converted for 'Nightstar' Channel Tunnel-related sleeping car service use and designated Class 37/6. New purpose-built rolling stock was also built but never used, the total project being shelved. Not even the main Dollands Moor yard was large enough to permit extensive marshalling and most changes in train formation to reflect the ultimate destination of wagons took place at Wembley and later Willesden. From the outside looking in it must have seemed to some commentators that the Brits could not manage a 'party' in a brewery!

Often overlooked is the huge amount of BR railfreight that was powered by electric locomotives, aside from the Class 92. One of the earlier trans-Pennine lines that almost exclusively used electric locomotives, albeit operating on a 1,500-volt dc system, was the Woodhead route. Class 76 locomotives, often working in multiple, hauled heavy trains between Lancashire and Yorkshire, with coal traffic dominating the scene. Sadly the entire route closed completely between Hadfield and Huddersfield Junction, Penistone, in July 1981 and the locomotive fleet was withdrawn.

On the London Midland Region early classes of 25kV ac overhead electric locomotives were often used on freight, particularly Class 85s. As the years went by and the entire Euston/Willesden/Crewe/Liverpool/Manchester/Glasgow routes were electrified, Classes 86 (often in double-headed mode) and 90 were increasingly seen on freight workings, and their travels were later to extend into southern East Anglia.

Other classes of 25kV electric locomotive could also be seen on freight from time to time, including the prestigious Class 90s. These locomotives were all reliable, although being only of a Bo-Bo wheel arrangement they could, on rare occasions in adverse weather, be found wanting on Shap and Beattock with the heaviest trains, mainly down to adhesion problems rather than available power. Many of these locomotives were taken into EWS and Freightliner stock following privatisation.

Although much was wrong with the BR goods and freight scene during the two decades following the 1963 Reshaping Report, as modernisation and massive transitions took place, a third star in BR's freight crown was the advent of the freightliner or 'liner' train envisaged by BRB Chairman Dr Richard Beeching and his Board. As already mentioned, initial thoughts of containerisation concerned mainly the domestic carriage of goods but what was to develop was a boom in particularly deep-sea international traffic that was perfectly timed to serve the requirements of a rapidly changing scene in world shipping.

Metal containers were becoming all the rage, whereby companies could load their produce, whether it be raw materials, manufactured goods or even personal possessions in secure boxes without risk of damage, contamination, pilfering or any other negative factor long-haul shipping might produce. Containers could be neatly stacked, easily loaded and offloaded not only to and from ships but also lorries. The dimensions were standard and considerable uniformity could be enjoyed, saving both time and money. The first freightliner as we have come to know them ran in November 1965 between London and Glasgow, and soon a domestic network grew up with 20 terminals in operation by the end of the 1960s.

One of the major innovations that assisted a large number of industries with transport infrastructure and rail connections was funding in accordance with the terms of Section 8 of the 1974 Transport Act. If certain conditions were satisfied money could be made available by way of a grant for up to 60 per cent of the capital cost of sidings, related signalling, handling equipment, access and storage areas, essential buildings and other related capital items. The bidding company had to demonstrate that there would be a significant movement in the transportation of its products or materials from road to rail and that any development in this direction was in the interests of the locality and/or its inhabitants.

In later years some funding was also provided by schemes promoted by the European Economic Community. This undoubtedly promoted freight by rail especially when the scheme was extended to rolling stock procurement. The first such grant was awarded in 1975 to Containerbase in order that they might develop their Aintree railhead. Within just over five years grants were awarded to 98 companies and their gross value was £29 million, allegedly increasing freight rail volumes by 19 million tonnes. Such grants continued through the years under a 'Freight Facilities Grant' label generally benefiting the rail industry. However, following the disastrous banking crisis of the 2009–11 period and a string of government expenditure cuts the scheme was

◄ In this Somerset quarry stone train scene from 1976, before the advent of air-braked wagons on such workings, a mottled Class 52 'Western' 2,700hp diesel-hydraulic, No D1065 *Western Consort*, leans to the curve at Crofton, just beyond Wolf Hall Junction, on the Berks & Hants route. Although 1976 was the locomotive's last year of service the twin-engined machine was going well with a heavy load of stone behind it in the shape of MSV-type vacuum-braked wagons, which were travelling up from Merehead Quarry. *Author*

axed in January 2011, leaving companies, logistic services providers and bulk hauliers to fend for themselves.

In typically muddled government thinking mode, while speaking 'with a forked tongue', this deterrent to rail transport was the exact opposite of their declared targets for achieving reductions in carbon emissions, which in 2011 seemed to be going out of fashion. Clearly the price of the grant exceeded the government's 'commitment to greener transport choices'. Ironically the decision impacted transport firms such as Eddie Stobart in that with draconian increases in diesel fuel charges they may otherwise, if grant aided, have been more likely to have increased their use of rail transport. But without financial assistance it would make it less desirable and more costly to invest in machinery and technology such as cranes and rail freight handling equipment. The devolved Scottish parliament hugely reduced the amount of their budget for such grants, but at least they retained a modest £2 million for the most deserving cases.

By 1970, about 140 freightliner trains per working day were operating over BR metals at speeds up to 75mph. However, after a promising start there was a period of stagnation when traffic levelled out, despite the growth of the deep-sea ports of Felixstowe and Southampton. The concept worked extremely well and it was merely a question of loadings to certain terminals that became a problem. From the mid-1980s to the early 1990s terminals at Aberdeen, Dudley, Dundee, Edinburgh, Holyhead, Hull, Longsight, Newcastle, Nottingham, Stratford and Swansea all closed. On the other hand, there were also a handful of new openings.

These freightliner terminals were divided into 'general use' examples and customer specific sites. The number of permutations of workings, theoretical and actual, was formidable and although the concept was great, by the last years of a publicly owned British Rail sector losses were being made. The business has since been financially turned around. However, the concept of containerisation was established and overall it, and that of the related intermodal method of operation, was an operational and financial success. One has only to see 10,000-tonne 'double stack' container trains crossing the USA to be convinced of a theory that has been put into practice, even though distances are of course much greater in the States.

There were many other success stories within the time frame under consideration. The volume of oil and petroleum products conveyed by rail in the late 1960s and early 1970s quadrupled from 5.2 million tonnes to 21.6 million tonnes per annum, but although many heavy block loads in the Petroleum Sector have survived the passage of time, the proliferation of oil pipelines and refinery-to-customer road transportation has had a negative impact, reducing annual tonnages by the end of BR to a modest 7.4 million tonnes. From the mid-1980s there were multiple oil terminal closures nationwide. It now seems rather strange that all of Gatwick Airport's fuel requirements are delivered by pipeline and to view empty sidings at locations as diverse as Galley Hill in East Sussex to Tiverton Junction in Devon. In the South East alone a dozen oil sidings, mostly used for local and domestic oil distribution, closed in the late 1980s and early 1990s. As already mentioned, much of this traffic went over to road transport rather than pipelines. This even included some BR depots, such as at Bristol Bath Road where the InterCity locomotive fleet fuel was delivered by road!

Although there were highlights in the goods and freight story in the 20 years following the Reshaping Report many of the negative aspects were not attributable to BR. British industry as a whole changed dramatically during this period. For many years there had been a lack of inward investment in many British industries that were soldiering on with outdated machinery and unsustainable working practices. Wherever one looked there was a lack of radical change as other developing countries gradually overhauled the UK as a top producer. Modernisation was urgently needed as industry went into loss-making mode.

When new machinery and working methods were introduced to make an industry more competitive there was always trade union opposition. In the railway world such issues as 'Driver Only Operation' where there was scope for nearly halving manpower in certain situations was resisted. The Railway Development Centre at Derby had developed a driverless remote control shunter but could not implement the change due to union resistance. For flimsy reasons ASLEF wanted to retain drivers' assistants if trains ran at over 100mph and there was a whole stack of other negativity, a fact not lost on freight customers.

In the car industry robotic assembly became uniform elsewhere in the world but in the UK there were mass walkouts at any sign of change that was likely to result in a reduction in manpower. In Fleet Street compositors were still moving around lumps of lead type when the age of computers and publishing software had arrived. On many occasions coal miners went on strike whereupon the government accused the unions of 'holding the nation to ransom', the worst dispute resulting in a three-day week for British industry. There were regular problems in the docks as well as restricted practices, including totally unacceptable nepotism and ridiculous lines of demarcation, resulting in the general public suffering from commodity shortages. In old-fashioned labour relations terms nobody wanted to return to Victorian times when company owners, bosses and 'big business' ignored all workers' rights and paid a pittance, but to demand more and more when the strikers were working in loss-making industries with huge deficits was short-sighted, unsustainable and suicidal, witness the current status of Liverpool or London Docks.

Although the mgr operation was an unqualified success the rest of the Coal Sector became a victim by the virtual disappearance of the domestic coal industry and by the decimation of deep-mining activities in the UK. From over 900 pits in 1948 to 600 in Dr Beeching's time, to less than 200 before the 1984/85 miners' strike, the industry was in turmoil. Eventually, the number of UK pits was reduced to a handful and general coal traffic in gross tonnage terms inevitably declined. Imported coal was on the increase and there was a small upside for BR in that much of it was rail hauled at some stage between the docks and customers.

The government created the British Steel Corporation in 1967, when 14 of the UK's major companies were brought into public ownership, which bizarrely benefited the industry by reducing or eliminating loss-making plants, thereby ensuring the survival of at least a streamlined industry within the UK. However, as with other large UK industries in the era there was a lengthy steelworkers' strike in 1980 and the unions shot themselves in the foot (and the foot of their railway colleagues) as rail traffic slumped by a massive 18 million tons. Following this commercial suicide, caused by a failure to understand worldwide commodity markets, together with a degree of intransigence, there was subsequently a number of entire plant closures and a radical reduction in the number of blast furnaces, from nearly 90 to just 15 by the end of the 1990s.

Plants from Workington to Shotton and from Brymbo to Ebbw Vale either closed or had their level of activity reduced. Britain's steel industry suffered from world overproduction and cheap foreign labour. Following a series of corporate takeovers and plant closures steel traffic by rail hugely declined. Again, imported iron ore, an essential industry raw material, was on the increase and as with imported coal much of this was rail hauled. Some modernisation took place but over the years the BSC workforce was halved and that was before later takeovers. Not all steel industry train flows were withdrawn and despite these reductions many regular workings continued throughout this period.

There was also a continuing traffic in other areas of the sector, such as scrap metal. It now seems remarkable that the vast plants of Corby, Consett and Ravenscraig are nothing more than a distant memory, at least to those who knew them in their heyday. A little metal tube activity survives at Corby but many sites have been completely razed.

Other types of goods and freight traffic such as cement, lime, sand, gypsum, potash, fly ash, china clay, liquid petroleum gas, nuclear traffic, armaments, timber and wood products, domestic waste, chemicals, automobiles, parcels and a whole lot more survived, some trains loading better than others. Most but not all of this traffic was conveyed by dedicated trains in block loads from terminal to terminal, fulfilling Dr Beeching's wish to encourage that sort of operation in seeking profitability and by exploiting what it was that railways did best.

However, many commodities were lost to the railways over time such as the transportation of livestock, milk and the movement of most perishable goods, while other traffic was lost because the costs associated with railway transportation became too expensive or too unreliable through regular disputes. By way of example a major loss was the distribution of newspapers, which left mostly London but also Manchester in their millions in the late evening or early morning for truly nationwide destinations. The author can vividly recall both BBC radio and television in Cornwall announcing on occasions that the newspaper train had broken down and the papers would be delivered late that morning. Unfortunately, this traffic was lost to road transport in the late 1980s, with the modern TNT logistics company being one of the beneficiaries. As we will see in a later chapter, most Royal Mail traffic would eventually go the same way.

The main casualty in the two decades following the Reshaping Report was wagonload freight. Such trains were always a delight for railway photographers because their length could never be anticipated, the mixture of wagons in the consist was seemingly infinite and they ran at fairly slow speeds. They often served small and sometimes ramshackle goods yards, they were aesthetically pleasing for the railway modeller, motive power was often old and British, they made a unique sound, especially the clattering of buffers and couplings when braking, and above all else those 'in the know' knew that such trains were doomed, always a magnet for the railway fraternity! As already detailed such trains were huge loss makers. They were slow, carried only part loads in old short wheelbase wagons, their braking was primitive, they required marshalling, often more than once, turn-round times were slow and hundreds of thousands of wagons were required to run the services.

As mentioned in the previous chapter, the BR network was full of ancient goods wagons that spent most of their time idle and when they did run they carried small loads over short distances at slow speeds. There was no doubt that road transportation was more suitable and cost-effective for the overwhelming majority of this traffic. Consequently, this source of traffic was attacked by putting up rates to a realistic level, avoiding outdated common carrier obligations, closing branches, minor lines and little-used stations (many of which had a working goods yard but with few wagons per week being loaded and/or unloaded), and streamlining traffic flows by having fewer marshalling and concentration yards. Minor loss-making traffic was abandoned if there was no opportunity of making such traffic profitable, despite the loss of customer goodwill. BR was largely successful in their quest and between 1968 and 1978 wagonload traffic declined from over two-thirds of total freight tonnage to just one-fifth.

With a concentration on block trains in fixed formations there was little need to marshal wagons and the huge yards that were constructed or modified as part of the Modernisation Plan became little used. Acres upon acres of sidings became weed covered and rationalisation was inevitable. Some yards were simply pruned while others were closed completely. However much BR pruned the system and discouraged hopelessly unprofitable loads it was not possible to ignore the still significant tonnages moved by rail under the wagonload label. In 1977, one of the more respected British Rail Chairmen, Sir Peter Parker, formally launched the new marketing name of 'Speedlink' that had its roots in the Beeching recommendations for 'bolting together' wagonloads to form complete trains that would run between major hubs. There would still be some 'tripping' to and from Speedlink hubs, but nevertheless there would be economies in running through but mixed trains over longer distances along the main railway arteries.

In the main, Speedlink services encouraged customers to use a new generation of air-braked wagons that could operate loaded at speeds of up to 60mph. As we will see in later paragraphs BR were partially successful. A major initial problem was that not all vacuum-braked wagons could be dispensed with as there were simply too many of them in service. This resulted in some duplication of freight services as both vacuum- and air-braked trains were obliged to operate over similar main line arteries. In the late 1970s and early 1980s the author will always remember the supervisors in St Blazey Yard in Cornwall finding out whether the 'air brake' was on time (by implication relegating certain other freights to lesser vacuum-brake status). Also for a while the initials 'ABS', for air-braked services, were part of the working railway vocabulary.

Throughout the country these old goods train relics from a bygone age eked out an existence but with losses continuing, and with BR wanting to encourage (some might say force) customers to sign up to Speedlink they closed the entire non-Speedlink wagonload business during 1984. From 25 trunk services running daily the new Speedlink network grew and the old traditional wagonload system gradually died a death. All manner of trainloads throughout the land were impacted by this decision but in pure financial 'bottom line' terms this was the right decision, there being

no room for romantics in business. A little of this wagonload traffic made the quantum leap to Speedlink but most was lost to the railways. BR tried really hard to grow tonnage and make a profit out of Speedlink operations and the national map of the Speedlink network began to look really impressive. The network even connected to Europe via the pre-Channel Tunnel Dover to Dunkerque and Harwich to Zeebrugge train ferries.

However, there was an irony in having such a comprehensive network in that as scores of terminals opened or were relabelled 'Speedlink' the system became more complex. As a consequence of such growth that complexity began to offend the rather purist views of the original plan of having only a handful of major arteries with a few key links running from operational hubs. In other words, Speedlink was beginning to resemble wagonload! Adding to the network complexity was a growing customer requirement for company sidings to be connected to the Speedlink network.

Growth was rapid and by 1980 12 main marshalling yard hubs, 20 lesser yards and over 200 goods and freight loading points were included in the Speedlink map. Geographically these ranged from Inverness, Aberdeen and Fort William to Stranraer and Carlisle, from Gateshead and Middlesbrough to Workington, Edge Hill and Holyhead, from Immingham and Norwich to Hereford and Carmarthen, from Sheerness and Dover to Wareham and Penzance, with a whole lot more in between including hubs in the Doncaster, Warrington, Birmingham, London and Eastleigh areas. While this growth might at a first glance appear to have been successful it quickly became clear that all of the old wagonload problems were a surviving virus in the still new Speedlink system.

Having quickly built up a comprehensive network much of the 1980s was spent analysing use and traffic patterns. As complexity increased so costly trip working also

▶ A scene that could hardly be more different compared with the previous photograph is this October 1986 study of General Motors Class 59 No 59003 heading a lengthy train of empty air-braked bogie hoppers that are returning to Merehead Quarry from Theale, seen approaching Fairwood Junction, Westbury. The new high-tech generation of motive power and the ultra-modern wagons are beyond comparison with the Class 52 and its vacuum-braked four-wheelers. Over time, 4,000-tonne jumbo stone trains would evolve, all as a result of private enterprise and inward investment in the railways. *Author*

increased. Wagon utilisation did not improve, in fact turn-round time was stuck at 11 days, a figure that was almost identical to those recorded in the days of Dr Beeching 20 years earlier. It became clear that losses were mounting, and within just five years of its launch another round of closures commenced. By the early 1990s there were only eight major yards in operation and approximately 100 active freight loading points. Under the sectorisation plans first announced in the mid-1980s Speedlink combined with Freightliner in October 1988, the new organisation being known as Railfreight Distribution (Rfd).

The shocking news was that Speedlink attracted £45 million worth of business per annum but in the process lost £30 million! This was unacceptable as the new business sector stood no chance of becoming profitable with the Speedlink millstone around its neck. As a result, every aspect of the business was examined to measure usage, efficiency, activity cost attribution, downtime, turn-round times, locomotive utilisation, staff utilisation, etc. The perhaps unsurprising result was that none of the Speedlink traffic flows paid its way. Even worse was the geographical distribution of customer sites, which precluded axing services in any particular area in an effort to save money.

There was no hope of any significant increase in Speedlink traffic volumes and little point in pruning the network and rationalising services. The fact was that overall journey distances were too small and trip workings carried too few wagons, the average being five vehicles. Marshalling and trip working accounted for a remarkable 80 per cent of total costs. It was calculated that to become viable the length of haul had to be 500 miles and that traffic flows needed to comprise at least ten wagon-loads per day, an impossible task in a country the size of Britain. There were ways of trimming costs such as ensuring drivers actually drove trains, as distinct from 'hanging around', improving turn-round times, ensuring locomotives were utilised more efficiently, reducing the amount of wagon marshalling, increasing the length of trains, etc. The inescapable fact was that the entire network, in total, carried only 2 per cent of national goods traffic and in freight-by-rail terms Speedlink carried an almost immeasurably small percentage of total UK freight.

Under the still new sectorisation business targets Rfd management were expected to deliver a 4 per cent return on asset value and with Speedlink included in the portfolio the startling recommendation was to discontinue the entire Speedlink service. The recommendation was accepted by the BRB in December 1990 and just seven months later notice was given to customers and the general public that from 7 July 1991 Speedlink would cease operations and all services would be withdrawn. Where Speedlink had handled traffic on behalf of other business sectors those sectors would become responsible for delivering their bulk loads to what were effectively their customers. Where loads could be regarded as dedicated bulk trainloads not relevant to Speedlink, but within the Rfd umbrella, they were to continue. Other aspects of sectorisation are detailed later.

Irrespective of the regional, functional or sector the gradual withdrawal of goods and freight services and the closure of lines and terminals radically impacted the BR network map. Significant parts of the country saw their total railway map shrink beyond all recognition during the two decades between the implementation of Beeching's recommendations, to the start of sectorisation. The companion volume *The Rise and Fall of British Railways: Branch and Minor Lines* features a considerable amount of information on line closures but specifically in terms of the goods and freight scene there was little to cheer about. Comparisons between the 1966, 1977 and 1988 gazetteers showed that over time a radical change for the worse had occurred.

To focus on just one industry, the network of lines serving the South Yorkshire, Nottinghamshire and Derbyshire, and South Wales coalfields was truly decimated, with scores of collieries and their associated lines and sidings closing and consequently being obliterated from the railway map. Loss-making pits, deep mines with geological faults, industrial disputes, North Sea gas, cheap imported coal, nuclear power stations, a downturn in the domestic demand for coal and increasing prices all contributed to the downturn of NCB collieries, negatively impacting their suppliers and the overall transport infrastructure.

It was not only the pits and their lines that closed but locomotive depots that served the industry, such as Shirebrook and Ebbw Junction. Even in areas not normally associated with heavy freight traffic, by way of example East and West Sussex, saw extreme rationalisation with the following closures in the 1970s and 1980s: Lavant (aggregates), Chichester (timber), Bartholomew's (fertilisers), Drayton (aggregates), Portfield (oil), Horsham (oil and fertiliser), West Worthing (roadstone), Beeding (cement, gypsum and coal), Hove (coal), Kemp Town (coal), Southerham (cement), Newhaven (aggregates and automotive), and Galley Hill (oil), although Chichester eventually reopened for aggregates and Crawley New Yard and Ardingly continued operations for stone traffic. Slightly earlier in the time frame, at the end of the 1950s and early 1960s, a large number of stations in East and West Sussex also had general goods and coal yards but by this time they too had already been added to the goods and freight closure list; a situation that prevailed nationwide as passenger car parking fees on former goods yard land greatly exceeded the income from a coal wagon or two.

There is little doubt that politically something more radical needed to be done to stem the losses being made by the railway. Some saw the answer as management accountability at an appropriate level. Hence in the early 1980s, a new organisational structure was established that saw the introduction of 'business sectors'. This would enable the BRB (and the government) to set specific financial targets against which performance could be measured. The sectors at that time were Freight, Parcels, InterCity,

Provincial and London and South East, but here we are only concerned with the non-passenger businesses.

Hints as to what might happen appeared in the BRB's Annual Report for 1979. Sector Directors were appointed and they were to conduct a strategic planning exercise and decide what could be afforded in terms of expenditure and investment. They were also to specify to regional general managers what standard of service they required. In the past there had been severe criticism of the complex and lengthy hierarchical management structure within BR but the BRB stated that sector management would introduce a sharper cutting edge in the battle to control costs and inject business criteria into a much wider range of decisions. The target for Freight was for it to be 'self supporting' by 1982, although later targets that were 'interim' called for covering two thirds of its then current cost depreciation. Unfortunately, there was a recession between 1979 and 1982 and any notions of the early interim targets being achieved would prove fanciful. In 1980, BR lost £76.9 million but due to yet more crippling and irresponsible strikes, mainly about rostering and manning changes, losses for 1982 rolled in at a staggering £175 million!

There was such intransigence in a series of negotiations between BR and ASLEF that on 25 June 1982 BR informed ASLEF that since negotiations had failed it would impose new rosters without union agreement. In response the union announced an indefinite withdrawal of labour from 4 July and a 14-day strike ensued. BR sought government support for their next move, which in the 'no nonsense' Thatcher years was freely given. On 14 July BR announced that from 21 July 1982 they would close down the entire railway system and sack the strikers. The poor old travelling public and commuter victims must have cheered or at least heaved a sigh of relief that somebody was on their side.

The union succumbed to pressure on 18 July and agreement to flexible rostering was agreed on 5 August.

ASLEF had lost this particular battle but they had stupidly damaged their own industry with the public and railfreight customers being mere victims as they were used as negotiating pawns. The author was commuting from the Sussex coast to London daily at this time and the union tactics were at times outrageous, such as working in the morning and then striking (or 'walking out') in the afternoon, leaving workers stranded in London. One can just imagine how BR's goods and freight customers viewed these stoppages, the unions having no commercial acumen whatsoever, apparently never asking themselves the question: 'Why would any manufacturer ship its goods by rail with seemingly endless strikes, in turn adversely affecting their customers and costing them money?'

If there was no freight then there would be no freight trains and therefore no train-driving jobs. It was hardly rocket science to work out. In a wonderful speech invoking what was known as 'the Falklands factor' the Prime Minister Mrs Thatcher stated that 'We are no longer prepared to jeopardise our future just to defend manning practices agreed in 1919 when steam engines plied the tracks of the Great Central Railway and the motor car had not yet taken over from the horse.' It should be clearly stated that a very significant minority of drivers had no interest whatsoever in striking but peer and union pressure was ever present.

The move to sector management was not universally popular and some regional managers expressed their misgivings. To them this was not some panacea to cure the ills of BR but added complexity to an already complex management system and structure. There was a tripartite management matrix of sector directors, functional managers at Headquarters and geographical regional managers. Finance and planning departments had to be reorganised to dovetail with the sector management approach. By 1982 progress was being made but as in the days of Beeching a 'bottom

▶ Although this interesting train is unidentified, the SR '5F' headcode relates to a Clapham Junction to Wimbledon via east Putney goods train. The fascinating 'rag bag' formation is seen threading the complex trackwork at Clapham Junction on 25 January 1980 behind Class 73/1 electro-diesel No 73101. These interesting locomotives could work under electric traction in 750Vdc territory, rated at 1,600hp, or under diesel power using an auxiliary 600hp English Electric engine on non-electrified lines and sidings.
Author

line' could not be established because of inadequacies in data collection. Furthermore, it was recognised by professional consultant accountants that the sector directors had insufficient authority. Even the experts stated that managerial authority within BR was 'diffuse and unclear'.

By 1985 sector directors were unhappy with the structure that had produced 'an ambiguous and confused matrix structure'. It is easy to forget that while this organisational mess was stumbling along, in operational terms all the usual goods, freight and parcels, trains were (perhaps surprisingly) working every day of the week, serving the customers of the railway. Also, there had been a short-lived 'localism' on the Western Region in 1985 with the creation of 'Cornish Railways', where local management had been given certain delegated responsibilities and targets. Certain marketing freedoms had also been granted to Scotrail.

With the introduction of the Class 58s a new Railfreight livery was introduced with grey bodysides, yellow cab ends, a broad red stripe at solebar level and large white BR double arrow logos on each side. The livery was later applied to most classes of freight locomotives. The early sectors continued but with the management structure being improved in 1985.

Within Railfreight the full 1986 sub-sector list was: Aggregates, Automotive, Building Materials, Coal Distribution, Coal Other, Distribution Services, Metals, Petroleum, Refuse and Freightliner. For Parcels the sub-sectors were: Premium Red Star, Newspapers and Post Office. London and South East was relaunched as Network SouthEast in June 1986 and a new 'Swallow' emblem for InterCity followed in 1987. As regards the freight sub-

sectors of the new Railfreight business, they were identified and given certain brand prominence. From 1988 a 'new' Railfreight livery was introduced to the locomotive fleet called 'triple grey' livery, incorporating colourful new decals and logos on the bodysides. These decals included, inter alia, Trainload Construction, Trainload Coal, Trainload Metals, Trainload Petroleum, Railfreight Distribution and Railfreight General. Within no time the original Railfreight locomotive livery became known as 'old' Railfreight livery. Losses continued and targets were adjusted, the return expected from the likes of Railfreight and Parcels being a 2.7 per cent return on assets before interest.

On the ground, in operational terms, the gradual introduction of more and more air-braked and higher capacity wagons saw most of the old vacuum-braked stock withdrawn, with, for example the final 450 china clay hood vacuum-braked wagons being replaced in Cornwall by 124 new CDA hopper wagons in February 1988. As previously detailed, the last of the 135 Class 56s was delivered in September 1984 and the last of the 50 Class 58 locomotives emerged from works in 1987, the same year as the tender for what were to become the Class 60s was issued to would-be manufacturers.

The older generation of British-built main line diesel locomotives were being withdrawn in ever increasing numbers as they became beyond economic repair. The last Class 46s were withdrawn in 1984, Class 25s and 27s were withdrawn in 1987 and but for a single example, the Class 45 'Peaks' disappeared in 1988. Serious inroads were made into the ranks of other surviving classes as freight traffic declined and short trip and wagonload freight ceased altogether.

▼ Varieties of shunting locomotive receive little publicity and yet for the whole lifespan of BR they were in a way the unsung heroes of the motive power scene. With the massive Llanwern steel works as a backdrop and with a mixture of colour light signals on the main line, and manual semaphore signals controlling the Uskmouth branch line, No 08780 heads towards East Usk Junction and Newport with some low-sided Railfreight wagons on 6 April 1988. Class 08 shunters were limited to 15mph but Class 09s had different gearing and could attain 27mph if necessary. Class 10s had the compromise maximum speed of 20mph. *Author*

1970s AND 1980s IN ACTION

▲ In this rather sad view from 1984 the track at Chinley has been severely rationalised, the signalbox has been made redundant and the island platform abandoned. Passing the dereliction and the weeds, a pair of English Electric Class 20s are seen heading downhill from Tunstead to Northwich with a load of limestone in old, 48-ton ICI vacuum-braked PHV hopper wagons. Some of these vehicles dated back to the 1930s and the third and fourth wagons still have the letters 'ICI' in place. *Author*

▼ Once steam traction was dispensed with the mainstay of freight operations in the Nottinghamshire and Derbyshire coalfields were Class 20s. These simple but effective locomotives were ideal for the freight movements of the day, particularly when working in multiple. Many of the class were gradually fitted with train air brakes to meet changing requirements. The combination of a 2,000hp output, a 144-ton gross weight and a total tractive effort that broadly equated with a single Class 56 or 58, they were a force to be reckoned with. On 12 November 1979 Nos 20135 and 20190 pass Coalville with a brake van to pick up a load. *Author*

▲ This 'modern' vintage scene recorded as recently as 3 March 1989 shows the classic pairing of two Class 20s taking to the sidings at Shirebrook East near Worksop with a couple of 'bass' wagons. Competing for attention with Nos 20004 and 20052 are two gantries of aesthetically pleasing upper quadrant semaphore signals. Except for the track itself all this infrastructure has now been swept away. The line peeling off to the left is the 'Robin Hood' line to Nottingham. *Author*

▼ Here we see a long rake of fully fitted mineral wagons, with not a brake van in sight, passing Melton Mowbray in a westerly direction on 4 June 1987, behind Nos 20032 and 20188. The tall cantilevered signalbox is of particular interest. The earlier locomotives were fitted with headcode discs as seen here, but later machines had a less-attractive headcode box fitted with roller blind letters and numerals. The class could work in multiple via a blue star coupling code. They were freight locomotives and not fitted with a train heating capability. During the mid-1960s they were the most reliable diesel locomotives on BR, and a total of 228 were built. *Author*

▲ One of the more interesting categories of non-passenger trains that has regularly traversed BR metals over many decades, has been the weedkillers. Although not 'goods and freight' as such, they should certainly be mentioned in this tome. Converted for push-pull working and reclassified Class 20/9, a batch of locomotives was converted for weedkilling services by Barclay of Kilmarnock. In May 1989, Nos 20901 *Nancy* and 20904 *Janis* cross the Lewes Road between Moulsecoomb and Falmer during their annual run with water tankers, the water being mixed with chemicals en route. *Author*

▼ In this truly magnificent study we see a typical Nottinghamshire colliery at Rufford, east of Mansfield. Nos 20151 and 20167 are seen shunting wagons in the sidings on 14 April 1977. One of the problems at such sites was the lack of modern loading equipment, which prevented the use of new-generation wagons. Of special note is an original Midland Railway signal, the shunter and the differences in wagon type. The 'main' line on the left is now disused, although after mining ceased in 1993 Rufford was used as a washery. A terrible disaster at the pit in 1913 claimed 14 lives. *Les Nixon*

◄ Class 20s were also used in many parts of Scotland, mainly in the lowlands but also on West Highland freights, as already featured. On 19 October 1984, the author found himself on the platform at Kirkcaldy in Fife as an engineers' train rolled into town behind No 20111. From the early 1960s, Polmadie depot in Glasgow had an allocation of Class 20s and in later years, many were based at Glasgow Eastfield, formerly sheds 66A and 65A respectively. *Author*

▶ An extreme photographic rarity was recorded on 10 November 1986 when one of the last remaining Class 25s was working north of the border. No 25057 had been working out of Carlisle and on this day it had been employed on the Dumfries to Maxwelltown trip with fuel tanks. The returning train is seen here at Dumfries goods yard. The line beyond Maxwelltown had closed to goods back in 1965 and the oil depot and the remaining line from Dumfries are now mothballed. *Author*

◄ Gradually the use of the traditional brake van for goods and freight trains evaporated and the train guard was obliged to travel in the rear cab of the locomotive. The weather at Dundee on 19 October 1984 was appalling as Class 26 No 26029 heading up empty coal wagons was brought to a halt at signals. Having just got the road the train moves forward towards either Perth or the Tay Bridge. The manual signals were swept away shortly after the photograph was taken. *Author*

▲ Saughton Junction west of Haymarket is where the main Edinburgh to Falkirk line diverges from the route over the Forth Bridge. Coming off the latter route on 26 February 1979 is No 37042 with a ballast train from Fife. Behind the locomotive is a contrast in ballast wagons ranging from the large bogie 'Seacows' to the much smaller, four-wheeled 'Dogfish' examples. *Author*

▼ Although the Class 37s were generally used as freight locomotives there were a number of significant exceptions. In fact, many of the class had train heating steam generators fitted for passenger train use. During the early 1980s, 31 members of the class were fitted with electrical train heating for passenger use as steam-heated rolling stock was withdrawn. However, this November 1986 photograph taken at Crianlarich shows the dual roles of the ETH-fitted 37/4 subclass. On the left, large logo No 37412 heads an up freight that had originated at Fort William while on the right, No 37411 powers away with a passenger train from Oban. *Author*

▲ About to enter Horbury cutting in Yorkshire, just east of the once-important Healey Mills yard, is No 25194 heading a short spoil train of used ballast on 20 August 1980. In the background is the site of Horbury & Ossett station, which closed in January 1970. The lines to the left are part of the abandoned route to Crigglestone Junction. Healey Mills's main claim to fame in more recent times has been its use as storage sidings for withdrawn locomotives, rather than a thriving freight marshalling yard. *Author*

▼ This view of the approach to Leeds City station on 26 June 1986 shows Nos 25313 and 25266 rolling through town with large bogie tank wagons, demonstrating in practice the theory propounded by BR in their Modernisation Plan of the 1950s, and subsequent Traction Plans, regarding the economic use of motive power. The idea in procuring large numbers of small locomotives was that they could be utilised singly on light trains or in pairs, working in multiple with a single crew, when heavier loads such as this were on the move. *Author*

► The Class 25s were widely travelled and eventually, after the North British Class 22 diesel-hydraulics were withdrawn, they found themselves operating in far-flung Cornwall. They were well suited to the Cornish branch lines and, again, could be seen double headed on heavier 'up country' loads. Passing the old Hallenbeagle engine house just east of Scorrier on 10 June 1980, is No 25225 with a Long Rock/St Erth to Exeter Riverside mixed freight, a phenomenon that is already history in west Cornwall. *Author*

▼ Contrary to the policy advocated opposite, this landscape photograph shows a weakness in the system, where a single 1,250hp Type 2 is allocated to a freight when a Type 4 would be more appropriate. The small, six-cylinder Sulzer was really struggling and was down to little more than walking pace as it crossed Ribblehead Viaduct and approached the signalbox at Blea Moor on 26 March 1982. The lengthy and loaded freight was 8M64 from Healey Mills to Carlisle. This was the last year of significant freight volumes over the Settle and Carlisle line as wagonload traffic was in terminal decline. *Author*

▲ It now seems unimaginable that this single coal wagon could be hauled all the way from the Midlands, via Shrewsbury, down to Machynlleth, along the Cambrian Coast via Barmouth to Porthmadog with no more than 14 tons of the black stuff on board. Even if part of a larger train earlier in its journey, the true cost must have been prohibitive. No doubt the train crew enjoyed their 'day out'. This Class 25 is seen passing Barmouth South signalbox as at least a dozen locals wait at the manual crossing gates for the Cambrian daily goods to pass in April 1975. *Author*

▼ In 2011, the embankment on the left of this picture at Buxworth, west of Chinley, fell into the road below, closing the line for several days. There were no such problems on 17 June 1983 when No 25035 hustled by with empty Blue Circle cement tanks that were destined for Earle's Sidings in Derbyshire's Hope Valley. The earlier batches of Class 25s had small centre windscreens because the locomotives were once fitted with cab end doors, which were later deemed to be redundant and plated over. *Author*

▲ Dr Beeching was a great advocate of the block load simply because it made economic sense not to be handling consignments such as this, which often needed to be marshalled into longer trains and then expensively tripped to customer yards and sidings. A regular for many years has been the Crossley Evans scrapyard traffic from their depot just south of Shipley. Hauling its load of twisted scrap metal east from Guiseley Junction in September 1986, is No 31187, the locomotive weighing more than its train. *Author*

▼ Even in its modern traction heyday, March in Cambridgeshire was the epicentre of East Anglian freight traffic. In addition to a junction station a sizeable motive power depot and the vast Whitemoor marshalling yard were nearby. Besides these there were extensive sidings to the east of the station. Add to that signalboxes, a triangular junction and a range of passenger services, time spent at the location by enthusiasts was always productive. With both colour light and semaphore signalling visible No 31229 rolls into the station from the Peterborough direction with a ballast train in February 1985. *Author*

▲ A Class 31 working where the locomotive was given a relatively high-speed workout was the 06.00 Plymouth to Old Oak Common empty newspaper vans. The train had travelled down from Paddington overnight taking the products of what was then Fleet Street to the West Country. The train is passing the wide platforms of the rationalised Newbury Racecourse station. Beyond the bridge in the background was where the old Didcot, Newbury & Southampton Railway briefly joined the Berks & Hants route. *Author*

▼ Whether such trains were economic to run or not, sights such as this are sorely missed on our railways. This up Didcot to Acton freight is vacuum fitted and 'modern' enough for the brake van to have been dispensed with. With a truly mixed load, including wooden-bodied box vans and Continental wagons, with a good sprinkling of coal hoppers, No 31305 tries to pick up speed as it makes its way along the up slow line at Moreton, east of Didcot, on 24 January 1980. *Author*

▶ A pair of Class 33 'Cromptons' had a combined power output of 3,100hp, although significantly less 'at the rail' and they were regularly entrusted with quite heavy trains. Thundering past East Worthing on the Sussex Coastway with a nearly 2,000-tonne Foster Yeoman stone train from Merehead to Crawley New Yard, are Nos 33028 and 33002, on 21 June 1982. The large air-braked 100-tonne bogie wagons were then new on the Somerset stone train circuit. In later years, Crawley traffic was tripped down from Acton. *Author*

▼ During December 1981 No 33012 emerged from Eastleigh diesel depot in a local version of the BR large logo livery, but without the large logo! The locomotive is seen here on 1 March 1982 in the company of a sister Class 33 leaving the sidings at West Worthing with empty grab-discharge stone wagons. During the 1980s the old disused goods yard had continued in use as a fairly short-term stone train terminal. The locomotives would run round at Worthing Central before returning to Westbury. A member of staff prepares to attach the oil tail lamp. *Author*

▲ Prior to the opening of the Channel Tunnel all rail traffic between the UK and the Continent had to use ferries, using mainly (but not only) the port of Dover. It was usual for trains to run on and off the ferry in parallel for weight balancing purposes over the hydraulic ramps. New Railfreight-liveried Class 33/2s Nos 33205 and 33206 propel chemical tankers and other air-braked wagons on to the SNCF *Nord Pas de Calais* on 13 February 1989. Lorries were carried on the upper decks of the ferry in this fascinating operation. *Author*

▼ One of thousands of freight services that no longer run is the Fawley to Tiverton Junction fuel tanks. The spread of pipeline networks nationwide and a growth in distribution by road has had a serious impact on the conveyance of petroleum traffic by rail. In the 1970s BR was carrying 20 million tonnes of petroleum products every year but within 20 years this had plummeted to 7 million tonnes. Rapidly approaching Castle Cary this Class 33/1 will be on the back run with these empty, large-capacity bogie wagons in 1979. *Author*

▲ This interesting train of nine PHA wagons is rolling down from the South Downs between Amberley and Arundel on 2 March 1983 behind 1,550hp 'Crompton' No 33065. The wagons had been in store at New Cross but they were being delivered to Chichester for use on the resuscitated Lavant to Drayton gravel trains, which continued to run until 1991. The headcode shows '9K', which is from Bricklayers Arms to Hove and Chichester via the Quarry line, and to that extent the train has been re-routed. The River Arun can just be glimpsed across part of the Duke of Norfolk's estate. *Author*

▼ Chichester goods yard in West Sussex has had very mixed fortunes over the years. In the 1930s it was a busy place where not only domestic traffic was handled but also loads destined for now long-closed Selsey and Midhurst branches. After closure as a general goods yard in the 1960s, it was used for wagon storage and civil engineers' trains. Following the 1987 hurricane, timber trains were loaded on the site and the sidings were used by recessed Lavant aggregate trains and fertiliser traffic for the nearby Bartholomew's siding. Following another closure it was resuscitated as a stone terminal for trains from Somerset. No 33004 is seen in the yard with some ancient ballast wagons in March 1983. *Author*

▲ Prior to January 1933, when the service was withdrawn, this old bay platform line at Botley was used by branch trains working to Bishop's Waltham. The line struggled on for goods traffic until April 1962. Now the surviving stub of the branch is part of a Foster Yeoman stone terminal. Having finished unloading its stone from Merehead Quarry this train will shortly return to Somerset. Getting into the cab of No 37272, with No 37271 in support, the driver will soon run the locomotives round the hopper wagons before the run to Westbury, on 5 March 1983. *Author*

▲ One of the great survivors in what was the Petroleum Sector is the weekly Fawley to Plymouth Laira and Long Rock, Penzance, oil train carrying diesel fuel for BR's own use. Entering Salisbury station with the loaded outbound train in July 1988 is No 37072, regarded as something of a rarity at the time. The only other liquid available nearby will be the beer and lager in the BR Staff Association premises in the left background! *Author*

▼ The rare sight of a Class 37 passing through St Johns station in south-east London on 15 January 1995 was down to engineering works at Plumstead. Petroleum Sector No 37220 was heading for London Bridge, where it would run round these side-discharge ballast wagons and continue to Hither Green. From there it would form the 12.00 departure to the possession site at Plumstead. The line to the right is from Lewisham. *Brian Morrison*

▲ Heavy trains of steel coil have been regular visitors to the old North & West route from Newport to Shrewsbury via Hereford for many years. They are relatively slow moving but the provision of good old-fashioned passing loops enables nimble diesel units to nip by. One such loop is located at the site of Wooferton Junction south of Ludlow. This Class 37 and its steel coil train is being held in the northbound loop in May 1988, but the passing passenger train is not yet in section, according to the GWR-pattern signals. *Author*

▼ In respect of most steel trains a single Class 37 did not have quite enough power, although in BR's final years some of the class had their generators replaced by alternators and lower-geared CP7 bogies were fitted, while another batch of 'heavy' freight Class 37/7s had 15 tons of ballast added to their weight to increase adhesion. However, for South Wales steel trains half a dozen locomotives had new engines and traction motors fitted and they were also weight ballasted, becoming Class 37/9s. The other solution in the quest for power was simple double heading, as seen on this steel coil working from Lackenby on Teesside passing Chesterfield behind Nos 37505 and 37510, on 4 February 1987. *Author*

▶ There was no need for the operators to worry about power output or ballasted Class 37s for this train. Lowly rated train 9P44 tiptoes through Newcastle Central comprising No 37015 and a standard 20-ton brake van during 1975, probably heading for Forth goods depot to pickup a local unfitted freight train. *Author*

▶ By the late 1970s the marketing name of 'Railfreight' was appearing in increasing numbers on wagon sides, the transfers incorporating the BR double arrow symbol. Passing Treeton Junction near Sheffield and taking the road towards Tinsley Yard is a Class 37-hauled down fitted freight on 15 November 1979. The lines to the right veer towards Rotherham. Sadly, these signals were swept away many years ago, depriving photographers of notice of the impending arrival of a train on this freight-only route. *Author*

◀ Class 37s in Cornwall had a reign over local china clay traffic of more than 20 years, from 1979 to 1999 inclusive. To make the transition from old vacuum-braked 'clay hood' wagons to modern air-braked CDAs in 1988 the locomotives needed to be dual braked. Running across Milltown Viaduct, between Par and Lostwithiel, in July 1986, is No 37135 with a load of china clay destined for the docks at Carne Point, Fowey. Note the difference between the flat-bottomed track on the up line and the old bullhead rail on the down road. *Author*

▼ This depressing but utterly fascinating scene shows the last knockings at Maesteg washery in South Wales, the year before the buildings were demolished. When photographed in April 1989 the washery had just six months of surface coal stocks left for removal. The site once received coal from Caerau, Coegnant and St John's collieries for washing but these pits closed in 1979, 1981 and 1985 respectively. Contrasting with the dull but intriguing surroundings is a brightly painted, new Railfreight-liveried No 37698 *Coedbach* that would shortly be leaving for Tondu. *Author*

▲ A further scene from the Welsh Valleys shows some open-cast activity at Nelson & Llancaich in September 1986. At head of a long line of 50-tonne HAA wagons, in a view looking in the direction of Ystrad Mynach, are Nos 37302 in blue livery and 37699 in original Railfreight colours. Once loaded the train will work to Aberthaw Power Station in South Glamorgan. *Author*

▼ Coal trains of any description are not normally associated with the southern portion of the Arun Valley, or Mid-Sussex line. However, on this day in February 1990, the main London to Brighton line was closed for engineering work and the returning Hove to Didcot coal empties were diverted. Nearing Amberley is No 37217 and a rake of empty HEA wagons that on the down run had contained domestic coal. Alas the working would soon become a casualty and by November 1990 it had passed into history as this type of network coal traffic was killed off, in the interests of reducing operating losses. *Author*

◀ It would appear that there is little money being made on this working as venerable Class 40 No 40057 passes the magnificent and lofty Chester No 2 signalbox with ten bogie flats in July 1983. The 1Co-Co1 veteran was making for Trafford Park to the west of Manchester. Chester General station is hidden from view behind the signalbox. The locomotive was withdrawn exactly a year later after a working life of 24 years. *Author*

◀ On occasions a train unexpectedly turns up that cannot be identified, unless the local signalman is available for interrogation. There was little chance of the latter in this case bearing in mind the distant and elevated position of Llandudno Junction signalbox, seen here. Nowadays there are websites-a-plenty and in-the-know gurus everywhere that can reveal such data, but on 24 June 1982 the originating point and purpose of this curious mix could not be determined and will remain a mystery. Arriving from the Bangor direction is No 40009, the last vacuum-only-braked member of the class then running. *Author*

◀ These elderly vacuum-braked flat wagons with white metal bearings were normally used for conveying lengths of rail and it could be that when photographed approaching Acton Grange Junction, south of Warrington, they were returning to Workington, but that is mere speculation. With white headcode discs glowing and without a headlight in sight this 133-ton Class 40 approaches from the Helsby and Chester direction and will soon be joining the West Coast Main Line. *Author*

▲ By 1983 the ranks of the Class 40s in active service were dwindling rapidly and the North West was the best place to observe and photograph the class at work. Whistling through the Manchester Victoria/Exchange complex on 17 June 1983 was No 40028 with a short, westbound goods. The platform on the right was reputedly the longest in the UK at 2,196ft. *Author*

▼ The 69ft 6in length of a Class 40 is very obvious in this view taken from the main signalbox at Shrewsbury. A commendably clean No 40182 crosses the lines from Wolverhampton as it heads down the Welsh Marches route bound for Tarmac's Bayston Hill Quarry, a few miles south of town on 14 September 1981. The ballast wagons are of the 'Mackerel' and 'Sealion' types. *Brian Morrison*

▲ Super power was provided for this prestigious freight train, the Horrocksford 'Ribblesdale' cement train from Clitheroe to Gunnie, near Coatbridge in Scotland, a 'new win' for the railways in 1982. On 26 March 1982, Nos 40181 and 40033 power their way through Kirkby Stephen 'wrong line' due to engineering works. The sound from their combined 32 cylinders made music in the hills on this cold still early morning; a truly magic moment. *Author*

▼ One had to feel sorry for this 2,000hp machine as it slogged over the Pennines with a load of Yorkshire coal for Lancashire. With a long rake of loaded HTV wagons in tow No 40157 is seen climbing into the 3-mile 64-yard Standedge Tunnel, where it would be spending the next ten minutes in darkness. Notice the abandoned tunnel bore on the left and the cascade of water upper right, not to mention the semaphore signals. *Author*

▲ This unusual track configuration at Skelton Junction was rarely photographed but all has now changed. Coming off the line from Warrington Arpley, which is no longer in use, is No 40035 with VGA vans. The route straight ahead once went to Glazebrook but that has also been abandoned. The surviving route to the right, which has now been singled, connects with the Old Trafford to Northwich line. As a result of these changes there is no longer a true junction at this location! This train is heading towards Stockport on 6 April 1984. *Author*

▼ Only Classes 60 and 66 now pass this spot at Great Rocks although by the time this appears in print Class 70s will no doubt be part of the scene. In March 1982, No 40094 is seen heading for Hindlow as it passes the approach roads for the massive Tunstead–Buxton Lime and Cement works. The train will reverse in Buxton and the old LMS-style brake van will then be at the back of the train. The dry-stone wall is in keeping with the area where manual signalling survives. *Author*

▲ Although the morning of 25 March 1982 had been fairly steady in freight traffic terms on the Settle & Carlisle line the middle of the day was immensely frustrating as a cloudless sky produced no trains for over two hours. However, the 'duck' was broken when train 8G15 Carlisle to Healey Mills appeared around the curve at Dent station mid-afternoon. In charge on this day was 'Peak' Class 45 No 45046, seen passing the by then disused signalbox. The lovely old station now offers 'B&B' accommodation for railway enthusiasts, and others. *Author*

◄ In this spectacular view the massive Durham Viaduct dwarfs the terraced houses of the ancient city as Class 45/0 No 45022 *Lytham St Annes* heads south with empty mineral wagons in the spring of 1983. The East Coast Main Line was eventually electrified and as a result overhead catenary now appears above the magnificent Victorian structure that dates back to the 1850s. Although the wagons are empty the exhaust reveals that the large, 1Co-Co1 is working hard. *Author*

▶ This elevated view of Sowerby Bridge in West Yorkshire shows the 'West' signalbox to advantage. Top centre is the station and on both sides of the line, but particularly to the left, there were once acres upon acres of railway infrastructure and sidings, including 25E engine shed in steam days. About to plunge into Sowerby Bridge Tunnel is No 45049 *The Staffordshire Regiment (The Prince of Wales's Own)* as it heads towards Hebden Bridge with a mixed goods, about 50 per cent of which comprises coal wagons. *Author*

▼ Running parallel with London Underground Limited tracks at West Ruislip with a load of old rubbish is this Greater London Council waste train working from what is now called the West London waste depot at Northolt, to Calvert waste disposal site. ETH-fitted Class 45/1 No 45117 passes lower quadrant semaphores on 14 December 1985 as it heads for Princes Risborough. Modern adornments such as a locomotive headlight in addition to marker lights were then appearing in greater numbers. *Author*

◄ Although Class 45 'Peaks' were widely travelled, in the minds of many their primary association will always be with the Midland Main Line from St Pancras to Nottingham, Derby, Sheffield and Leeds. In that scenario, No 45120 is on home ground as it accelerates past Wigston South Junction, south of Leicester with an up van train. There are lines of coal wagons behind the signalbox and in March 1983 semaphore signalling was extant. The line to the left connects to the Leicester, Nuneaton and Birmingham route. *Author*

◄ Chemical, bitumen and oil tanks are joined by a scrap wagon and coal empties as a wonderful old-fashioned freight rolls off the distant Pennines at Sowerby Bridge. Old textile mills compete for attention with modern apartment blocks, with unfortunately the former losing out in terms of scale. Based on the position of the distant signal this eastbound train has the road towards Greetland Junction and Healey Mills, where it is no doubt destined. Again, a Class 45 2,500hp 'Peak' is the favoured power, this time No 45020. *Author*

◄ Although it has only eight bogie wagons in tow the train weight will be considerable as steel bars head south near Littleworth, south of Worcester, behind No 45046 *Royal Fusilier* on 14 August 1978. The train will travel via Gloucester and Chepstow ending up at one of the South Wales steel processing plants. The 'feathers' on the colour light signal will activate for trains travelling via Abbotswood and Norton Junctions into Worcester Shrub Hill. *Author*

▲ The shadows are lengthening on a quite delightful evening as the Plymouth to Leeds parcels train approaches Standish Junction, a few miles south of Gloucester. On 3 August 1983 No 45129 was providing the motive power for just five vans. The double track top left is the 'Golden Valley' route that climbs into the southern Cotswolds via Stroud and Kemble to reach Swindon. *Author*

▼ Cousins of the Class 45 'Peaks' were the 1Co-Co1 Class 46s, the main difference being that the latter had Crompton Parkinson traction motors and generator, compared with the Brush electrical machines on the former, although both shared the Sulzer 12LDA28B 12-cylinder diesel engine. Heading an express parcels train in the twilight hours at Paddington in 1977 is No 46016 that was finally withdrawn in December 1983, and cut up at Swindon the following year. *Author*

▲ The time is 23.26 according to both the magnificent Victorian timepiece on Platform 1 and the modern electric example on Platform 2. Class 47 No 47247 has a 17-minute wait before it disappears into the night with train 3B10, the 23.43 Paddington to Plymouth vans. The DMU is 2B64, the 23.59 departure for Reading General, no doubt hoping to sweep up the last of the late-night revellers. Note the large number of BRUTE trollies on the right, which the parcels will have briefly travelled in. *Author*

▼ Having already featured Chester No 2 signalbox at the east end of the station area, here we illustrate the unusual Chester No 6 signalbox at Chester South Junction. Taking the 15mph-limit freight-only spur from the Hooton direction and heading for either North Wales or Wrexham is No 47266 on 13 July 1983. In the background is the DMU depot and the CE Plant Distribution centre. *Author*

▲ Kensington Olympia is a great place for freight train fans because the variety encountered is seemingly infinite and one never knows what is going to round the bend next. On 29 May 1987 it was an automotive working that rattled past on the down through road, which judging by the Continental van and the Peugeot cars had originated in France. Providing the power was No 47085 *Colossus*, one of the named Western Region examples. The line has since been electrified and the track layout changed. *Author*

▼ The casual observer may be worried that they are suffering from triple vision, judging by the number of brake vans bringing up the rear of the ten-wagon 7V00 train from Carlisle to Severn Tunnel Junction. About to plunge into the 1-mile 869-yard Blea Moor Tunnel on the Settle & Carlisle line is No 47149 on 26 March 1982. Note the plantations of conifers that have been planted on the bleak hillsides. *Author*

◀ Over the years the main GWR artery between Birmingham, Oxford and Reading has become a regular stamping ground for Freightliner trains from the Midlands, the North and Scotland to the Southampton area. In the mid-1980s it was very easy to become somewhat blasé about drab all-blue Class 47s, which were not only numerous but which had a virtual stranglehold on such container workings. No 47320 threads Harbury cutting with an up train. *Author*

◀ It looks as though heavy oil trains have, over time, had an adverse effect on the roof of Bournemouth station, but it has in fact it looked like this for many years. One of the few trains that at the time did not stop at the station was the Furzebrook to Eastleigh bogie tanks entrusted on 27 August 1988 to No 47123. Unfortunately oil, liquid petroleum gas and ball clay trains from the Wych Farm/Furzebrook area have now all ceased, leaving a very sparse freight scene in this part of Hampshire. *Author*

◀ A true anachronism and, even in 2012, an oasis reflecting the infrastructure of a bygone age persists at Marchwood on the Fawley branch line from Totton, west of Southampton. On 7 October 1989, light engine No 47256 is held at signals for the signalman to manually open the crossing gates, whereupon he will return to the box, pull off the signals, wait for the locomotive to pass, reset the signals and reopen the gates; not a place to be caught in your car! The Class 47 will pick up a load at Marchwood MoD depot and take it to Didcot via Eastleigh. *Author*

▲ Another truly wonderful survivor in 2012 is the delightful all-over roof at Frome station in Somerset. Although the track has been heavily rationalised the main building remains; in fact at the time this Class 47 and brake van were photographed in the early 1980s the station had just enjoyed a repaint. The town is served by Bristol to Weymouth passenger trains but most freight traffic uses the main Frome avoiding line. *Author*

▶ A truly British freight scene on 8 August 1988 (8/8/88!) with a Class 47 on loads at an obscure Sussex siding, with a fine cathedral spire in the background and the Union flag proudly flying. The scene is Bartholomew's agricultural produce siding to the east of Chichester, now sadly disused. The main traffic was fertiliser from Ince & Elton. The empty train would travel to Barnham, where the locomotive would run round before disappearing westward. *Author*

◄ This view is no longer possible due to major road improvements, which is unfortunate because it shows the remains of Shawford Junction where the old Didcot, Newbury & Southampton Railway joined the LSWR main line. The old trackbed can just be detected on the right. Heading south to Southampton Maritime Freightliner depot is No 47019 in original Railfreight livery. By the end of the 1960s the domestic system had grown to 20 Freightliner terminals and by 1970, 140 Freightliner trains per day were working over the BR network. However, some train loadings were light and there followed a period of rationalisation, including a number of depot closures. *Author*

◄ Recovering from a signal check on the approach to March is No 47348, in February 1985. The train will pass through the junction station to Ely North Junction where it will travel north to King's Lynn. The locomotive will then run round these 38-tonne PAA wagons before continuing to the British Industrial Sand installation at Middleton Towers. The sand is mostly used in glass-making. *Author*

◄ Over recent decades there has been spasmodic freight traffic at the East Sussex port of Newhaven. Loads have included sea-dredged aggregates, Ford Transit vans and trials with Freightliner containers, but none came to fruition in terms of regular long-term rail traffic. At Newhaven there are stations at Newhaven Town and Newhaven Harbour, which are both on the Seaford branch line (seen on the left in this view), but in the right background is the little-used Newhaven Marine station, which, ironically, is adjacent to the Channel ferries. Leaving Marine in December 1989 with flat wagons is No 47337 *Herbert Austin*. *Author*

▲ The history of Class 47s is long and complex and is described in the companion *The Rise and Fall of British Railways: Main Line Diesel Locomotives*. However, despite trials and tribulations, modifications, the introduction of subclasses, the application of over 300 livery variations and enough renumberings and renamings to fill a book, they were the mainstay of BR mixed-traffic operations for decades. Passing Aller Junction signalbox south of Newton Abbot in 1986 is Class 47/4 No 47515 with what is thought to be a Plymouth to Leeds van service. *Author*

▼ Well away from the main line is Railfreight Distribution Sector's No 47258 seen here propelling old vacuum-braked HTV coal hoppers into the Rugby cement depot at Chinnor on the old Princes Risborough to Watlington branch line, on 20 December 1989. This was to be the last inbound service before the line closed. Latterly, the imported coal came via Newport Docks. Passenger services ceased back in July 1957 but, happily, the line was later taken over by preservationists who now operate it as the Chinnor & Princes Risborough Railway. *Author*

▲ Although the English Electric Class 50s were designed as express passenger locomotives the boffins clearly had a part-time mixed-traffic role in mind as the locomotives were fitted with automatic slow-speed control for operating merry-go-round trains. From new, they had numerous other novel electrical systems, which added considerable complexity compared with their DP2 predecessor. From the start they worked a number of LM Region freight services but one of the less-usual diagrams was the WR Kensington Olympia to St Austell Motorail trains. On 19 June 1982, No 50030 *Repulse* passes the site of Defiance Platform near Saltash in Cornwall with the return 14.50 from St Austell. *Author*

▼ Later in their careers a number of Class 50s were displaced by High Speed Train units and gradually they found themselves working almost demeaning trains. In revised Network SouthEast livery No 50017 *Royal Oak* gently smokes its way off the Okehampton and Meldon Quarry line at Crediton to join Barnstaple branch metals with a 950-tonne ballast train, on 20 October 1988. The train would reverse in Exeter Riverside yard before heading 'up country'. *Author*

▲ In this 34-year flashback some of the last six-wheeled vehicles to run on BR are featured, the time-honoured 3,000-gallon milk tanks that worked from various West Country and West Wales sites to the Capital. These wagons originated at St Erth, Dolcoath and Lostwithiel, the train being the 16.10 St Erth to Acton milk. Headed by No 50010 *Monarch* the train is passing below the ancient remains of Restormel Castle a couple of miles south-west of Bodmin Road in Cornwall, on 11 June 1978. *Author*

▼ This returning empty newspaper van train from Milford Haven to Old Oak Common was a monster, loading to 15 bogies. Booming up the climb towards Patchway on the English side of the River Severn is a somewhat grubby No 50024 *Vanguard* on 6 April 1988. On the down run the train will have supplied much of the South and West Wales population with their morning read. The up and down roads slightly separate at this point, through Patchway 'old' and 'new' tunnels. *Author*

◀ By the time the first of the new Class 56 locomotives had been delivered it had been 15 years since BR had made any meaningful investment in new-build freight locomotives and as a result technology had been static. The reliability of ageing machinery was, understandably, beginning to deteriorate to unacceptable levels. The answer was a new procurement for 3,250hp Type 5 Co-Cos that turned the scales at 126 tonnes. On 2 July 1988, No 56063 *Bardon Hill* passes Winchester with a diverted 09.55 Loughborough to Ardingly stone train. *Author*

▼ Passing the lock on the Kennet & Avon Canal at Little Bedwyn in July 1989 is No 56065 with empty Tiger POA box wagons bound initially for Westbury. The first 30 Class 56 locomotives were constructed in Romania under Brush oversight. In total, 135 locomotives were constructed but unfortunately, despite all the lessons of the past, they were not trouble free. The locomotive here is in Railfreight Construction livery and was part of the FALX Freight (Aggregates) Leicester Area Pool. *Author*

▲ From a lineside photographer's perspective in the late 1980s the goods and freight scene on BR was changing. The old ramshackle mixed-goods workings slowly declined as gradually larger and larger air-braked wagons that were the basis of the favoured block load consist came on stream. When these Bardon aggregate bogie wagons are compared with the goods trains illustrated in the early pages of this book the difference is remarkable. Heading east through Ruscombe, near Twyford, is large-logo No 56047, on 27 September 1986. *Author*

▼ There were few trains on the BR network that required double-headed Type 5s but one of them was the Port Talbot to Llanwern iron ore working. The available 6,500hp (less at the rail) would not be required on this down run with the returning empties, seen here at Pyle, near Margam, behind Nos 56048 and 56050 on 19 June 1986. Two Class 56s had replaced triple-headed Class 37s, but a long series of changes within the industry resulted in the trains being phased out. *Author*

▶ It can be argued that without any shadow of doubt the most innovative and profitable use of bulk freight haulage have been the merry-go-round (mgr) pit-to-power station coal trains. The almost continual use of modern freight rolling stock with minimum down time, loading and unloading on the move, using modern motive power with (mostly) slow-speed control and compatible equipment to maximise system throughput, have all contributed to an extremely efficient operation. An all-blue Class 56 heads south through Normanton in 1983 with well-loaded HAA wagons. *Author*

▶ Merry-go-round trains were less common on the Southern Region but there were a handful of regular flows. One such working is shown here with No 56087 heading train 7O85, the 13.25 Toton New Bank to Northfleet, passing between Bexley and Crayford in Kent on 2 July 1987. These trains normally loaded to between 32 and 40 HAA wagons, each with a gross loaded weight of 50 tonnes. In later years there were minor variations of the basic wagon, which included improvements to the braking system. *Brian Morrison*

▼ Between 1965 and 1983 a staggering 11,000 HAA-style wagons were constructed and the last examples were still in operation in 2011, although most had by then been replaced by large, lightweight aluminium bogie wagons with more than twice the payload of their four-wheeled predecessors. Keeping some 1,900 tonnes on the move on the approach to Chesterfield in February 1987 is No 56092 of the FEYA Freight (Power Station Coal) Yorkshire Class 56 Pool. *Author*

▲ This shot of Cresswell Colliery gives a good impression of the infrastructure required for the then modern mgr trains to be loaded. Most of the coal-fired power stations had a continuous loop of track to facilitate unloading but most collieries had loaders that were either located over sidings adjacent to main lines or at the end of dedicated branches. Here, No 56020 positions wagons under the loader in 1979. In common with a large number of Nottinghamshire collieries Cresswell closed in the early 1990s. There was a terrible underground fire at Cresswell in 1950 when 80 miners perished. *Author*

▼ Coal Sector decals on this Class 56 give a clear indication that this up mgr train at Worksop on 3 March 1989 is being properly employed. Unusually on this day a succession of five up mgr trains were all Class 56 hauled, their numbers being 56006/11/15/18/23, all of which were built in Romania! The semaphore signals and the sidings on the left were uprooted many years ago. Even though passing coal trains, to West Burton and Cottam power stations, are now thinner on the ground it is still possible to have a superb breakfast at the cafe/buffet on Worksop station, hopefully between freight workings. *Author*

▲ The 50 Class 58s followed the Class 56s in chronological terms. They were of a simpler construction and similar to Class 20s (and to American locomotive practice) in that they had narrow bodies, external walkways with side panels to access equipment. They were fitted with 12-cylinder Ruston Paxman engines delivering 3,300hp. In as-delivered original Railfreight livery No 58028 scampers past Hinksey Yard, south of Oxford, with a load of coal for Didcot Power Station in July 1988. *Author*

▼ The scene is Blackwell Junction on the Erewash Valley line in August 1985, now over a quarter of a century ago, and just a few months after the end of the disastrous year-long coal miners' strike. Class 58 No 58015 is shunting some empty HAA coal wagons that will later work to one of the nearby pits; probably Sutton Colliery. New Hucknall, Pleasley and Teversal coal mines had already closed in 1982, 1983 and 1980 respectively. In the right foreground are the Nottingham and Toton to Chesterfield main lines while in the background a single track veers off towards the old Westhouses depot. *Author*

▲ An optical illusion is at work here because at a glance No 58022 would appear to be hauling a truly massive load whereas two mgr trains are in fact passing each other at Worksop East on 3 March 1989. Although the use of domestic coal had been in decline for years, even mgr coal traffic was slowing at this time as the closure of loss-making UK pits accelerated. Depending on one's point of view, this was the result of either political dogma or the self-inflicted wounds of the coal miners' strike. Increasing volumes of coal were being imported which, according to the power generators, was cheaper despite being shipped, in some cases, halfway around the world. *Author*

▼ By 1989 No 58001, the first member of the 50-strong fleet and by then one of the FENA Freight (Power Station Coal) Nottinghamshire Class 58 Pool, had been repainted in new Railfreight triple grey livery with Coal Sector decals applied. Having supplied Ironbridge Power Station with coal the Type 5 is seen returning with the empties at Madeley Junction, where it will join the Shrewsbury to Wolverhampton main line. *Author*

▲ This quartet of photographs shows different stages in the developing Somerset stone and aggregate freight-by-rail business. Back in 1976, Class 52 diesel-hydraulic No D1001 *Western Pathfinder* rolls off the Merehead branch at Witham with a long line of loaded vacuum-braked MSV wagons. The train has the road and will now join the up main line to Westbury. These twin-engined 2,700hp machines found regular employment on such trains, especially once they had been demoted from Class 1 express passenger train employment. However, they would become extinct in BR service by February 1977. *Author*

▼ By the beginning of the 1980s the customers in the shape of Foster Yeoman and Amey Roadstone Corporation were expanding rapidly, but they were fed up with having to rely on ageing and unreliable BR motive power. Various remedies were tried, including the employment of pairs of 2,700hp Class 50s on heavy stone trains. A trial was conducted on 3 March 1980 using two locomotives hauling a massive, 3,300-tonne stone train and a test coach, which is seen here passing Clink Road Junction on the outskirts of Frome behind Nos 50024 *Vanguard* and No 50021 *Rodney*. The trial was unsuccessful in that the train suffered from coupling failures. *Author*

▲ Eventually, BR decided to utilise their latest freight locomotives on the Somerset stone workings and a number of Class 56s were based at Westbury, although formerly allocated to Cardiff Canton. They had the grunt to operate reasonable loads singly but their reliability left much to be desired. With 43 wagons each weighing in at 50 tonnes gross, No 56031 *Merehead* powers eastward between Clink Road Junction and Fairwood Junction in 1984 with a Foster Yeoman load from Merehead. However, there were about to be significant motive power developments in the Somerset hills. *Author*

▼ In one of the most dramatic moves during the BR years the Foster Yeoman company, which had already procured an American-built switcher at Merehead Quarry, were light years ahead of parochial UK thinking and decided to take the radical step of purchasing their own locomotives from General Motors in the USA. They had to endure all the BR Technical Centre ballyhoo and the usual trade union issues, but four locomotives duly arrived in 1985 in a blaze of publicity. Dubbed the Class 59s they were a resounding success. On 17 September 1986 No 59003 *Yeoman Highlander* is seen at Bradford Junction signalbox with 6A67, a Merehead to Wootton Basset stone train, which will take the single line via Melksham. *Author*

▲ Even back on 29 July 1980 St Leonards (Warrior Square) station in East Sussex was not noted for its non-passenger workings. Nevertheless, there could be nothing more delightful exiting Hastings Tunnel than two old Southern Railway wooden-bodied utility vans forming a returning empty newspaper train headed by Class 73 electro-diesel No 73125. Headcode '22' signifies a Hastings, Battle, Orpington to Charing Cross routing duty. *Author*

▼ On 17 March 1983 there were problems on the Coastway West line in the Barnham area and the Eastleigh to Norwood Junction freight was brought to a stand at Woodgate crossing. The infrastructure dates this scene, with old manual crossing gates, diminutive crossing signalbox and an old cast-metal Southern Railway 'Beware of Trains' sign for intrepid pedestrians. No 73133 waits patiently for the road; time for the crew to catch up with the daily paper, or the special traffic notice! *Author*

▲ This attractive sylvan setting is at Brandy Hole Lane crossing; 'crossing' in terms of a run-round loop rather than a road. This was the scene in November 1984 on what was once part of the old Chichester to Lavant and Midhurst branch line. Except for a centenary special and an occasional railway enthusiasts' Chartex the last passenger trains ran in 1935. On 20 November 1984, and with autumn in full flight, No 73123 propels its wagons down to an aggregate loader at Lavant. When loaded it will depart for Drayton to the east of Chichester. *Author*

▼ You could wait a long time for a freight train in this car park at Southwick, unless you were aware that the Hove to Didcot coal empties were being diverted on the day in question. Running westward along an embankment in February 1984 is No 73136 with a rake of empty HEA coal wagons. Although now a pensioner, the author was, perhaps, once a boy racer with his red Ford Fiesta XR2 in view; a great vehicle for getting that second shot! *Author*

▲ It was not often that the opportunity arose for making a picture featuring a trio of the now long-extinct Southern Railway wooden-bodied bogie utility vans, but this image, taken in absolutely torrential rain in the bay platform at Barnham in West Sussex on 21 August 1983, was irresistible. Class 73/0 'JA' No 73004 was at the head of the empty newspaper vans that had delivered the Sunday papers to this part of the county. It would soon return via the Arun Valley or Mid-Sussex line. Alas, neither the locomotive, the wagons, the working nor the bay platform have survived the passage of time. *Author*

▲ Several photographs of newspaper trains have been featured in this part of the chapter because for decades they were an integral element of the freight and parcels operating statistics, and because in certain parts of the south they were the only non-passenger trains running. Under the all-over station roof at Brighton there is plenty of motive power about just to handle a couple of vans. No 47537 had arrived with the vans and No 73134 was about to depart with the 17.58 return working to London Bridge, on 29 September 1988. *Author*

▼ If you are a lover of impressive statistics then the Ouse Valley Viaduct, north of Haywards Heath on the London to Brighton main line, is for you. Built in 1842 the structure is 170 years old and yet, today, an estimated 110 trains still cross the structure every day. It is 1,475ft long, 96ft above the ground, has 37 semi-circular arches and comprises 11 million bricks. Crossing the impressive structure on 13 June 1988 is No 73134, seemingly a regular on the Brighton to London Bridge vans. *Author*

▲ For many Northerners one of the great tragedies was the closure of the famous 'Woodhead' route between Penistone and Hadfield, first to passengers in January 1970, and finally for freight in July 1981. Although the route was electrified it was incompatible with modern electrification schemes and also it was, in the broadest sense, a duplicate route over the Pennines. On 24 February 1981 Nos 76032 and 76034 draw to a halt at Wombwell Main Junction for bankers to be attached for the ascent of Worsborough Incline. *Author*

▼ The Class 76 1,500V dc electric Bo-Bo locomotives were originally known as EM1 class. The 58 locomotives were built at Gorton by Metropolitan Vickers and except for the original prototype were introduced from 1950. They weighed just under 88 tons. High up in the bleak Pennines Nos 76011 and 76015 pass Torside signalbox with a good load of scrap iron for Yorkshire, on 25 February 1981. *Author*

▲ The Class 76s normally worked over the Woodhead route double headed, particularly after being fitted for multiple working in 1968. Bearing in mind the locomotives were the equivalent of Type 2 diesels, with a continuous rating of only 1,300hp, that mode of operation was understandable. Travelling through the snow at Deepcar are Nos 76006 and 76024 with a Rotherwood to Deepcar coal train. Note the double pantographs on each of the locomotives. *Author*

▼ When descending from the Pennines, often with heavy loads, the Class 76s would take advantage of their regenerative braking system. On 26 February 1981 Nos 76032 and 76034 climb through Crowden towards Woodhead with empty HAA mgr wagons from Fiddlers Ferry Power Station west of Warrington. This traffic would soon be travelling over the Standedge route behind diesel locomotives rather than behind these 30-year-old 'sparks' machines that would soon become redundant. *Author*

▲ The West Coast Main Line has always been an important artery for freight but pathing restrictions over some sections of the route have resulted in much of the traffic moving at night. Although electric traction was commonplace, where trains were using only part of the route, diesel traction predominated. A train that required superpower was the British Steel Corporation's Ravenscraig to Shotton working and here we see Class 87 No 87023 *Highland Chieftain* supported by a Class 86 passing Winnick Junction, north of Warrington, where diesel power would take over. *Author*

▼ As time went by both BR and their customers realised that carrying cars in any form of open wagon with its many attendant risks, including severe weather and stone-throwing vandals, was not a good idea. Gradually, wagon design improved leading to the total covering of the payload as seen on this 'Silcock Express' working, entering Bletchley from the south behind old-timer No 85026 on 31 January 1987. *Author*

▲ During the past decade the railways of Stratford in east London have changed beyond all recognition caused by track realignments, the arrival of the Docklands Light Railway, the construction of Stratford International, and High Speed 1 plus former BR station rebuilding. In this flashback to 'old' modern times Nos 37263 and 37116 head towards Channelsea Junction and Willesden with bogie flats. The lines to the left go to Temple Mills Yard. *Author*

▼ Continuing with the 'under the wires' theme is this interesting photograph of 8F21, a sand train from Oakamoor to St Helens where its contents will be used in the manufacture of Pilkington glass. No 25210 and a sister locomotive are seen at Winnick Junction where they will leave the West Coast Main Line. Notice the sand blowing out of the wagons, BR using both MTV and HKV types for this traffic. *Author*

▲ Deepcar station on the old Great Central Railway line between Sheffield Victoria and Penistone closed way back in June 1959 and now it is the terminus of a freight-only line from Woodburn Junction, Sheffield. In days when the line continued through to Penistone No 37054 runs through the snow beneath the old Woodhead route 1,500V dc overhead lines with an up ballast train headed by a 'Shark' brake van. *Author*

▼ A final glimpse of diesels under the wires is this study of a pair of 'Choppers' headed by No 20112 passing Elsecar Junction between Barnsley and Wath, with slow-moving coal train 8M17 on 24 February 1981. It is hard to believe that there is now no railway at all at this location and Wath Yard is but a distant memory. *Author*

▲ The tide is in and the water level in the River Fowey is high as the flagship of the Cornish Railways Class 37 fleet, No 37207 *William Cookworthy*, is reflected in the water as it leaves Lostwithiel for Carne Point, Fowey, with a load of china clay on a most delightful spring day in 1986. The freight-only line lost its passenger services in 1965 but is still used for china clay, albeit less frequently than it was in this era. *Author*

◄ It was always refreshing to photograph any locomotive that was not all-blue in the 1970s and '80s. Looking surprisingly fresh in this 1974 view at Iver, Buckinghamshire, on the GW main line, is green-liveried Class 31 No 5812, with full yellow cab ends. The (mainly) coal train 8A77 is on the up slow line because it is a lowly rated Class 8 train, which is on its way initially to the nearby West Drayton coal concentration depot. *Author*

◄ It is June 1972 and BR/Sulzer Class 25s have replaced North British Class 22s on the Culm Valley milk train working. Imported from the London Midland Region, No D7502 (later to become No 25152) has retained its green paintwork and is seen approaching Culmstock with just three empty six-wheeled milk tankers in tow. This traffic to Hemyock in Devon lasted until 31 October 1975, passenger services having been withdrawn in September 1963. *Author*

◄ Far away from the South West is this scene on the southern fringe of the Lake District. Heading down express parcels train 4P24 near Grange-over-Sands on Morecambe Bay, is this early-series Class 25 in the summer of 1973. The train has a mix of four-wheeled and eight-wheeled vehicles behind it, and the next stop will be Barrow-in-Furness. *Author*

▲ With the background totally dominated by the eight vast cooling towers of Ferrybridge Power Station, grimy all-blue No 31178 heads north at Broughton with a ballast train on 17 April 1984. Ferrybridge 'C' is the third power station built in the area, superseding older plants. It produces 1,955 megawatts of electricity and is what is known as a multi-fuel site, where there has been an increase in the proportion of biomass used in its boilers, thereby reducing coal consumption. *Gavin Morrison*

▼ A busy scene at Clay Cross Junction in June 1985 finds an intriguing event taking place as loaded mgr power station coal trains are using both the up and down main roads on the Erewash Valley route. Slow lines are on the far left, while diverging to the right are the lines to Derby and beyond. No 58015 in new Railfreight livery is heading north towards Chesterfield. Introduced from 1983 the 50-strong class were victims of the downturn in the coal industry and of the privatisation of BR. EWS inherited the Class 58s but their sights were on new procurements from North America. Some of the class were later successfully employed in mainland Europe. *Author*

◄ A stirring spectacle on the wilds of Rannoch Moor finds No 37026 leaning to the check-railed curve as it heads south from Corrour and approaches Rannoch Viaduct with this 18-wagon Mallaig Junction to Blyth Alcan bauxite empties on 18 June 1985. The Class 37s replaced Classes 26 and 27 on the West Highland lines from 1981 and enjoyed motive power domination until 2005. They were more powerful and more reliable than their predecessors while retaining an acceptable route availability rating. *Rail Photoprints*

◄ With the beautiful hills comprising the Long Mynd as a backdrop the British countryside is seen at its best at Marshbrook, just south of Church Stretton in Shropshire. Heading south on 6 May 1988 is a heavy Shotton, Dee Marsh Junction to Llanwern steel train headed by a very special locomotive, one of the re-engined and ballasted Class 37/9s. No 37903 is in original Railfreight livery, the locomotive having been fitted with an eight-cylinder Mirrlees 1,800hp engine and other associated equipment in a 1985/86 refurbishment. The Class 37/9s were allocated to a special Metals sub-sector pool based at Cardiff Canton. *Author*

▲ These platforms at March station are no longer used by passengers, since services to Wisbech and Spalding were withdrawn in 1968 and 1982 respectively. Creeping around the curve from Whitemoor Yard is No 37058 with what appears to be two goods trains: a four-wagon domestic coal train and brake van, and an engineers' train with old track panels and spoiled ballast, also with its own brake van. The latter can just be seen at the top of the photograph. Note the freshly replated and repainted panels on the leading cab end, with marker lights over the old route indicator boxes. *Author*

▼ This scene from 5 August 1977 now looks particularly dated and shows the situation then prevailing at hundreds of old, unmodernised collieries, where loading was slow and primitive and where the National Coal Board used BR wagons as storage bunkers, drastically reducing turn-round times. The colliery is at Clayton West at the end of the 3½-mile branch line from Shepley, south of Huddersfield. The colliery opened in 1879 and closed in 1983, the same year as the branch passenger service. No 37040 of Healey Mills depot is seen shunting elderly wagons.
Gavin Morrison

▲ This photograph illustrates an era when various classes of BR diesel pioneers, such as this pair of ageing Class 20s, were being replaced by new Type 5 Class 58s. With two shiny new 'predator' machines lurking in the background, Nos 20008 and 20186 depart the yard at Blackwell Junction, just north of Westhouses on the Erewash Valley route, with a dozen loaded southbound HEA coal hoppers from Sutton Colliery, on 19 June 1985. *Author*

▼ Although primarily pairs of Class 20s were employed on coal trains they could turn their hand to other tasks, such as Metals Sector workings, one of which is seen here heading south through Chesterfield in August 1987. After extensive reorganisations within the British Steel organisation to reduce losses in the early 1980s, all primary steel-making was focussed on six locations: Ravenscraig, Redcar, Lackenby, Scunthorpe, Llanwern and Port Talbot. Some plants closed altogether while others were reduced to secondary activities and status. Rail traffic plummeted but recovered somewhat in the early 1990s, only to decline again. *Author*

▲ Just prior to the Type 5 locomotive revolution in the quarries of Somerset during the mid-1980s, British-built motive power dating back to the 1960s was employed on Foster Yeoman and ARC stone trains including Classes 33, 37, 46 and 47. A glowing No 33020 and sister locomotive No 33038 are seen powering a loaded Yeoman working comprising PGA wagons through the scenic Wylye Valley south of Warminster, on 28 May 1985. Other changes were afoot at the time including the gradual replacement of these four-wheeled hoppers to PHA and PTA bogie wagons. *Author*

▼ Although at the time there was a single 'up and down' locomotive-hauled commuter train from Uckfield to the Metropolis on Mondays to Fridays, by the August 1985 date of this picture, hauled trains, especially non-passenger workings, on the line south of Oxted were an infrequent occurrence. This engineers' train from Three Bridges via Croydon was being positioned at Crowborough & Jarvis Brook in readiness for weekend track work and is seen leaving Eridge behind No 33032. Note the 'stunted growth' signal gantry with two up home signals thereon. *Author*

▲ The last of the famous Class 42 2,200hp Maybach-engined 'Warship' diesel-hydraulics was withdrawn in December 1972, a year after their Class 43 relations. No 818 Glory was withdrawn in November 1972 and the author was extremely fortunate in finding the beast on domestic coal train 6O81 at Salisbury in August 1972, shortly before its demise. After withdrawal the locomotive languished at Swindon Works for several years before being cut up. The alloy nameplates applied to these locomotives now sell for thousands of pounds at auction. *Author*

▼ Following the demise of the twin-engined 'Warships' in 1972 it was the turn of the versatile single Maybach-engined 1,700hp 'Hymeks' to be gradually withdrawn following the BRB decree that diesel-hydraulics belonged to the ranks of the 'non-standard'. Although never renumbered, the locomotives were to become Class 35s under the TOPS computer system. Although the majority of the 101 locomotives were withdrawn in 1971/72, some staggered on until 1975, when they too became extinct. During the autumn of its life, No D7026 is seen at West Drayton coal concentration depot with a mixed load. The locomotive was cut up at Cohen's scrap yard at Kettering in January 1977, 27 months after withdrawal. *Author*

▲ Completing this double-page spread of Western Region diesel-hydraulic locomotives working freight trains is this study of one of the venerable and much-missed Class 52 'Westerns', the 'Rolls-Royce' of the WR fleet. Approaching Wolf Hall Junction near Savernake is a very clean No D1030 *Western Musketeer* with a long line of empty stone wagons returning to Westbury during August 1974. Demonstrating its versatility, No D1030 had previously been diagrammed for 1A55, a Penzance to Paddington express, at least according to the headcode blind! *Author*

◄ Back in August 1972, now 40 years distant, this blue Class 73 electro-diesel, No E6035 (later No 73128) using electric traction, is seen passing West Worthing with a Bricklayers Arms to Chichester via Hove van train. Just visible in the up sidings is a 4-COR electric unit, the type having worked the 'Portsmouth Direct' line since the late 1930s before ending their days on humble Coastway stopping services. *Author*

◄ An immense improvement in livery terms was when some of the rather box-shaped Class 73s appeared in BR large-logo blue livery. In October 1986, an immaculate Class 73/0, No 73004, one of the original 1962-built batch of half a dozen locomotives that were designated 'JA', was captured on film arriving at Southampton from nearby sidings with an up van train for postal traffic. As can be seen from the signal identifiers, the whole of the signalling in the Southampton area is controlled by Eastleigh panel, some six rail miles distant. *Author*

◄ A further Class 73 livery development saw some of the class painted in InterCity livery although once the IC Swallow livery emerged some referred to this paint scheme as 'Mainline'. No 73123 *Gatwick Express* was relegated to breakdown train duty on 1 November 1986 as it passed Goring-by-Sea in West Sussex with a heavy crane and support vehicles. The locomotive later became No 73206 and was employed in push-pull mode on 'Gatwick Express' services, thereby justifying its name. *Author*

▶ Although perhaps not strictly in the goods and freight category, an interesting locomotive allocation in the late 1980s and early 1990s was the resident 204hp shunting locomotive normally stationed at either Sandown or Ryde St John's on the Isle of Wight. Absolutely glowing in its new BR blue livery is No 03079, seen in the old island platform at Sandown in June 1989. IoW freight traffic had ended in the 1960s but the little shunter was used mainly on engineers' trains. It was formally allocated to the DCSD Eastleigh and Ryde Depots Shunting Locomotive Pool. *Author*

▶ This interesting old transparency has been included because it shows Class 37 No 37104 with two ballasted brake tenders working freight 7V50 on the down fast line at old Oak Common. The slow-moving train would shortly use the crossovers to get it out of the way of fast-moving express trains, but also to enable it to access Acton Yard. The train will have originated on the Southern Region and travelled via Kensington Olympia, North Pole and Old Oak East Junctions. *Author*

▶ A unique experiment in Railfreight locomotive development terms occurred in 1987 when a single member of the 50-strong Class 50 fleet was selected for conversion to Class 50/1, the main feature being a bogie change to sacrifice top speed for power at slower speeds. After initial trials, No 50149 *Defiance* was exiled to Devon and Cornwall where for about 18 months it served the china clay industry. In February 1988, the locomotive is seen leaving Parkandillack with a mixture of air- and vacuum-braked wagons for St Blazey. Within a few days all the clay hood wagons would be withdrawn. *Author*

▲ Another freight train with three brake vans bringing up the rear is seen rounding the curve into Inverkeithing station from the Kirkcaldy and Thornton Junction direction on 10 August 1983, behind No 26026. What is so fascinating is that despite the passage of time and the introduction of train identity headcodes the driver has still taken the trouble to display a single disc beneath his cab showing this to be a 'freight, mineral or ballast train stopping at intermediate stations (or a branch freight train)'. The lines bottom left go to Dunfermline and beyond. *Gavin Morrison*

▼ This fine example of an Anglo/Scottish Freightliner working on 2 June 1978 shows early versions of the modern metal containers that we are now all familiar with. Nearly all are marked as Freightliner boxes with not a shipping line or international carrier name in sight. Rolling along the cliff tops at Burnmouth and passing a cluster of gorse bushes in bloom and a single grazing sheep is BR blue No 47270, one of the class delivered new to Haymarket in 1965. *Gavin Morrison*

▶ Traditionally the north-east of England has been a focal point for goods and freight traffic, although in recent decades there has been a significant decline in volume as British industry and the UK's manufacturing base has changed in profile. On 22 August 1981, No 40087 passes Bensham, just south of King Edward Bridge Junction, with the Leith Docks to Tees Yard empty bogie bolsters, after delivering another load of pipes for the then growing North Sea oil and gas industry. *Anthony Guppy*

▶ About to take the single-line token at Leek Brook Junction is the driver of Nos 25269 and 25282 on 8 June 1984 as the Class 25 duo make for Stoke-on-Trent with a sand train from Oakamoor. This is now all part of the Churnet Valley Railway network, which offers a 27-mile round trip and subject to a successful new share issue, is expected to expand further towards Leek and Stoke in the future years. *John Chalcraft/Rail Photoprints*

▲ When photographed in September 1986 this was the latest thing on the stone and aggregates railway scene, with a nearly new GM Yeoman Class 59 hauling air-braked hoppers running on roller bearings with rapid discharge hoppers. However, the wagons were gradually phased out in favour of bogie wagons. Mendip Rail Ltd was formed in October 1993 when the rail resources of Foster Yeoman and ARC Southern were combined, while within the industry, takeovers and amalgamations subsequently continued apace. This resulted in further locomotive livery changes. In the late afternoon light this up train is seen passing Wanstrow on the Merehead branch with the locomotive in FY blue and silver livery. *Author*

▼ Once squadron IC125 services took over nearly all of the long-distance Class 1 passenger trains in the West Country, surviving Class 50s, were mainly employed on passenger trains between Waterloo and Exeter via the 'Southern' route, but they were also put out to grass somewhat on lesser workings. Crossing the splendid Coombe St Stephen Viaduct between St Austell and Truro is a dirty No 50006 Neptune with the returning empty Chacewater to Plymouth Friary and Plymstock cement tanks in April 1985. *Author*

▲ This photograph is the epitome of the vision that BR bosses had for their regenerated freight services in the mid-1980s; an immaculate new Railfreight-liveried locomotive with distinctive branding coupled to smart new large-capacity, air-braked private owner wagons, in this case English China Clay slurry tankers. Looking quite magnificent in this official shot at Blackpool clay dries at Burngullow in Cornwall is No 37672, later named *Freight Transport Association*, and five blue bogie tankers. *English China Clays Group*

▼ This illustration shows an interesting period when new bogie hoppers were being delivered, but not in sufficient numbers to make up complete trains. This train at Westbury in 1985, hauled by large-logo-liveried No 56048, comprises a mix of both bogie and older four-wheeled hoppers. The leading PHA bogie hoppers were part of a 1984 order from Procor for 37 purpose-built aluminium-bodied wagons; however, there were structural problems leading to costly maintenance and by 1989, after only five years in service, they had all been withdrawn. *Author*

▲ Although Guide Bridge to the east of Manchester is still an important junction station its status pales into insignificance compared with 1979 when this photograph was taken. One of the downgradings was attributable to the closure of the Woodhead route in 1981 and a subsequent general downturn in freight traffic in more recent times. Passing extensive overhead 'knitting', EM1 Class 76s Nos 76027 and 76026 pass Guide Bridge with a coal train. *Gavin Morrison*

▼ The London Midland Region West Coast Main Line ac electric locomotives must not be forgotten as they performed tirelessly on goods and freight trains, not only between London and Crewe and later Glasgow, but on associated routes to Manchester and Liverpool. All the early types such as Classes 81 to 85 are now extinct on BR metals, but here we have a reminder of happier times with No 81002 approaching Basford Hall near Crewe with northbound British Oxygen Company bogie tanks on 31 May 1983. *Gavin Morrison*

BR SECTORS IN THE 1990s

THE SEEMINGLY NEVER-ENDING organisational changes did not stop with the arrival of the 1990s. During 1990 there was a further shift in structure when the Railfreight business was divided into Trainload Freight and Railfreight Distribution. The former comprised most bulk traffic, which included Coal, Construction, Metals and Petroleum, whereas the latter included Freightliner and the Speedlink network, as well as certain Chemical, Mineral and Automotive block loads. The management of these two main divisions must have considered the split grossly inequitable because at the time of the reorganisation Trainload Freight made a profit of £132.8 million on a turnover of £516.7 million whereas Railfreight Distribution was the poor cousin losing £73.4 million on a turnover of £176.7 million.

As already detailed, by 1991 the hugely loss-making Speedlink business had been killed off after a life of 17 years. However unrealistic the government's expectations were the Ministry of Transport was in no mood to relax pressure on the BRB to increase financial performance and for 1992/93 they imposed a £50 million profit target for Railfreight or a 4.5 per cent return on estimated asset values, with the Railfreight Distribution side of the business targeted to break even. The Parcels sector had an ambitious £9 million profit target. A problem compounding all these various calculations, assumptions and targets was that the country as a whole was in a period of recession, with the barometer of house prices having dropped significantly from the late 1980s.

In fact, from 1988/89 through to 1993/94 Railfreight Distribution turnover dropped by 26 per cent, Trainload Freight by 34 per cent and Parcels by a whopping 51 per cent. This situation made nonsense of the stringent 1989 targets, which could not, in the circumstances, be met. Extraneous forces were also acting against the railways such as the fallout from the steel industry in 1988, the electricity generating industry in 1991 and finally the coal industry in 1994, the latter after very significant rationalisation in just about every respect, but especially pit closures. All of these massive industries were large customers of BR's trainload business and any reduction in traffic for whatever reason would obviously impact the profitability of goods and freight services. Considerable cost-cutting took place on the freight side of BR but the primary changes involved a fundamental shift whereby instead of the government investing in the railfreight industry through BR it became expected of industry, the actual customer, to provide private capital for purposes such as wagon procurement and infrastructure. As a result, Trainload Freight's £136 million operating surplus for 1989/90 dropped to £68 million in 1991/92 and to about £45 million for 1993/94.

Railfreight Distribution, which was targeted with breaking even on its operating costs, lost a fortune, from £65 million in 1988/89 to a staggering £152 million in 1990/91. Ironically, this massive loss was incurred in the first year of RfD operating as an independent business. After Speedlink was axed these losses reduced to 'only' £119 million in the following year! This axing presented a special problem in that BR had signed up and made commitments to Eurotunnel about engaging in the wagonload freight and intermodal businesses, which to some extent conflicted with the plans to rationalise the UK freight business.

BR undertook to provide sufficient infrastructure by the date of the tunnel opening to provide for 5.2 million tonnes of non-bulk freight and 2.9 million tonnes of bulk freight, a commitment backed by both the English and French governments. How would this non-bulk freight be handled if there was no Speedlink network to move the wagons? Although Speedlink was abolished in 1991 it was overlooked that over 70 per cent of the former Speedlink traffic was retained in contracted trainloads on services that were dedicated to a particular industry or customer. Also, RfD was trying hard to develop its deep-sea Freightliner container traffic focussing particularly on Felixstowe and Southampton, but also planning for what was hoped would be a growing Channel Tunnel intermodal business. Again, forecast traffic failed to materialise in the volumes envisaged and by 1998, over four years after opening, less than half the anticipated traffic volumes had been achieved.

Returning to organisation there was frantic activity within the corridors of the BRB following the presentation of the Railways Bill in January 1993. The railways had to be organised in such a way that the structure was commensurate with plans for privatisation. This was immensely complex and furthermore the number of permutations was seemingly infinite. There were repeated discussions about a regional approach, a sector approach, an all-embracing single entity approach, a return to the 'Big Four' type of structure, etc. To give just a small insight into their deliberations, items for discussion and consequently decision included formulating policy, rail regulation, restructuring issues, system access, franchising (passenger services), contracts, networking, safety, contracting out, management chain, international services, freight, parcels, rolling stock ownership, staff pensions, and a whole lot more.

The Chairman of the BRB stated that it was the intention to make shadow appointments to the track authority and operating companies as soon as possible and to settle all new structures by 31 December 1992, to identify the best structure for freight and parcels by 31 March 1993, and to effect the separation of BR's track and operating by April 1994. There were many hundreds of meetings between managers, members of the BRB, the Ministry of Transport and other interested parties. The effort was mind boggling in that below a senior Project Management Group there were 12 working groups, each handling a particular major aspect of privatisation. A series of consultation documents were produced. Chris Green of InterCity expressed his concern at the 'levels of bureaucracy currently emerging'.

The wrangling, committee referrals, government impositions and downright opposition to privatisation has filled a number of books, and suffice to say for our purposes that the Railways Act was passed on 5 November 1993, there having been over 500 amendments made just by the House of Lords as it passed through the two houses. The Act had increased from 158 to 244 pages in size as it passed through the various stages within the legislature! One of the first acts, effectively creating a 'shadow' company was the creation of Railtrack in November 1993, and establishing that organisation as a wholly owned government company from 1 April 1994. Railtrack was to own the infrastructure but also to maintain and renew all civil engineering work, signalling, telecommunications, electrical equipment and fixed plant items.

In general, in a lead-up to privatisation from 1990, there was yet another wide ranging review by Trainload managers of their businesses and the prospects were generally gloomy. There was some cash generative traffic and a generally profitable core business sector, such as power station coal, aggregates, steel, refuse, etc., but non-core and cash neutral loads, such as domestic coal, cement, finished steel and most petroleum/oil traffic, were to be discouraged by cost cutting and discriminatory pricing. Capital assets were much reduced within the 1988/89 to 1993/94 timescale, with the freight locomotive fleet being reduced by 50 per cent, the freight wagon fleet by 40 per cent and manpower was reduced by 20 per cent. By the time privatisation took place annual freight traffic by rail within the UK had fallen to under 100 million tonnes, a reduction of 50 per cent in just 20 years. The railways were then conveying just 4.5 per cent of the nation's goods and freight.

The sale of various elements of the erstwhile BR structure produced many problems, including the privatisation of Rfd, which did not occur until 21 November 1997 when EWS took it over; see below. Rail Express Systems was separated from BR and sold as a separate business, albeit after a new Post Office contract was negotiated. However, it would be September 1995 before BR could get rid of Red Star. As for Trainload Freight the new 'shadow' operating units created with imminent privatisation in mind were

geographically based being Loadhaul (north-east), Mainline (south-east) and Transrail (south-west). To the layman these labels seemed rather strange, the assumption being that certain parts of the UK, other than those mentioned, had no freight trains whatsoever!

These changes gave rise to another round of livery changes or at least the application of logos and decals. This all added to the 'spice of life' for the railway enthusiast, especially the photographic brigade. These companies were offered for sale in 1995 but yet again a disagreement in approach between the BRB and the Ministry of Transport resulted in them being acquired for a very modest £225.15 million on 24 February 1996 by a single purchaser, a consortium led by the American train operator Wisconsin Central, which also later bought RfD and, as stated above, Rail Express Systems.

In the year prior to purchase Loadhaul handled 38 million tonnes of freight with a £150 million turnover, owned 194 locomotives and 5,470 wagons. Mainline carried 29 million tonnes, had receipts of £136 million, with 284 locomotives and 6,203 wagons, while Transrail conveyed 23 million tonnes of freight, with a turnover of £127 million, owned 436 locomotives and 7,637 wagons, these figures reflecting the nature of their respective businesses. The CEO, Ed Burkhardt, made some quite radical announcements regarding modernisation including the purchase of 250 new heavy freight locomotives from General Motors in North America and the early withdrawal of dated British Classes 20, 33 and 37 and the 'ageing and unreliable' Class 47s. There would be other large investments all round including a major new build in respect of their inherited wagon fleet.

The company seemed very proactive and created a new livery, which was launched at Toton in April 1996, surprisingly applied to old stager No 37057. They adopted the name of English Welsh & Scottish Railways and operated 85 per cent of all British freight trains between 1995 and 2007 when, on 28 June, the EWS company was acquired by Deutsche Bahn AG of Germany. DB also acquired the Spanish Transfesa company at the same time. The rebranding with the marketing name of DB Schenker occurred from 1 January 2009, but this is all well outside of the remit of this volume. It should be added that following privatisation a number of other freight operators appeared on the scene and 'open access' arrangements would see other smaller companies enter the fray, while some fell by the wayside.

Organisations such as the Rail Freight Group were formed to promote the freight operators and they were the source of some interesting statistics. They pointed out that since privatisation private sector investment in rail freight has exceeded £1.6 billion, enabling rail to capture 11.5 per cent of UK surface freight transportation. The freight operators had invested in over 400 brand-new Class 66 locomotives and over 3,000 freight wagons. They added that a single freight train could remove 50 heavy goods vehicles from the road, that in the past six years rail freight had removed 31.5 million lorry journeys from the roads and that every tonne of freight carried by rail produces 80 per cent less carbon dioxide than by road.

Furthermore, rail freight transported coal that produced 25 per cent of the UK's electricity and 80 per cent of stone used in construction projects in London, and 20 per cent nationwide. RFG claimed that Marks & Spencer, Superdrug, Argos, ASDA, Safeway (pre-takeover), Tesco and Rosebys were just some retailers using rail freight. They also claimed that Ford, Nissan, Volkswagen UK and MG Rover (as it was) also used railfreight to transport their products. The port of Felixstowe had now grown to handle 250,000 containers for rail transportation per annum and that Southampton was running at a rate of 1,000 containers per day. Above all else efficiency had been hugely improved since the days of BR in that manpower had been reduced by 30 per cent but turnover volumes had increased by 50 per cent, this fact being a poor indictment of BR.

Prior to looking a little more closely at the various commodities carried on UK railways it should perhaps be mentioned here that the very last train to run under the auspices of good old British Rail was the 23.15 freight train from Dollands Moor to Wembley on 21 November 1997, hauled by No 92003 *Beethoven*.

Parcels Sector was a disaster in business terms. From 4.5 per cent of total railfreight traffic in 1988/89 this fell to 2.5 per cent in 1993/94. The sector failed to meet targets and turnover decreased from £125.5 million in 1988/89 to just £78 million in 1993/94, a 50 per cent reduction in real terms. In 1991/92 the small sector lost £30 million, an unsustainable figure and a business that was unlikely to attract bidders in the condition it was then in. Years earlier in the early and mid-1980s, BR had already withdrawn from the general collection and delivery business as well as the Royal Mail parcels business. The author can vividly

remember the down 'Premium Parcels' workings out of Paddington in 1979/80, which often comprised a Class 31 locomotive and just a single van.

Contracts with the newspaper industry for distribution by rail also came under pressure from the mid-1980s following litigation, with courts finding in BR's favour. Nevertheless, all newspaper traffic ceased in November 1988 as road transport offered far greater flexibility and reduced costs, an irresistible combination. Eventually the Parcels Sector, which by then comprised Red Star and Royal Mail letters, was re-branded 'Rail Express Systems' (RES). Long contractual negotiations with the Post Office followed, with BR attracting a higher income estimated at 20 per cent in real terms, but in return the Post Office demanded a better quality of service. The deal included compensation payments if BR failed to deliver.

In part BR did fail to meet service targets and in 1989/90 compensation payments amounted to £1 million, and £0.5 million the year after. There were squabbles in pricing, especially in calculating Parcel's share of fixed costs and the form of payments for the use of passenger trains. In the medium term both sides invested in the business with the customer paying over £100 million for a new special and purpose-built hub at Willesden and a fleet of new dedicated parcels trains. Eventually, after a protracted series of events BR tried to sell off the parcels business but they initially failed, although the loss-making Red Star business was eventually acquired privately following a management buy-out for a nominal sum in September 1995. RES was finally sold to EWS in November 1997.

Following the abandonment of Speedlink one of the great surprises in 1994 was the creation of an almost nationwide 'Enterprise' network by the shadow Transrail company. As already mentioned, although the Speedlink wagonload traffic and marketing name were abandoned

▶ One of hundreds if not thousands of goods and freight workings that have ceased during the 1948 to 1997 BR years is the Ripple Lane to Portfield, Chichester, fuel tanks. Having used electric traction while on the main line, immaculate Departmental grey No 73136 has used its auxiliary diesel engine to propel the wagons into the oil depot. The train will return as 7Z00, 16.08 Chichester to Redhill empty tanks, on 8 March 1990. Note the catch point in the foreground. *Author*

in 1991, being hopelessly loss making, not all of the traffic disappeared, especially where certain commodities or specific companies contributed sufficient rail traffic to form trains that were effectively block loads. Transrail looked at ways in which the methods of operating employed by Speedlink could be improved and streamlined, thereby reducing costs. The ratio of trip working on a ton/mile basis was closely examined, the theory being that to convey just a couple of wagons a very short distance as a feeder service was acceptable, but the greater the distance of the trip the larger the load and therefore the income had to be. They made less use of marshalling yards. There were also overlaps with Trainload and Mainline where appropriate, but with EWS acquiring all three major UK shadow freight companies such dovetailing became much easier.

Services improved and many were speeded up including 75mph running on the West Coast Main Line, resulting in a London to Glasgow timing of eight hours – quite respectable for a freight train. The Ministry of Defence trains were included in the Enterprise system providing even more route permutations. Eventually a number of former trainload customers and their loads were integrated into the Enterprise system that continues to this day. Although the Enterprise network is not the same as the old wagonload and Speedlink operations it does provide a transport and distribution system by rail for smaller loads, insufficient to form block trains, from a wide range of customers that otherwise would have no alternative to road transport.

There is a vast, indeed almost infinite, range of goods and commodities carried by rail in the UK. Every variety of trainload has its own story to tell with the opening and closing of railheads, changes within the business, amalgamations and takeovers, changes in public demand or government policy, changes in technology, companies growing or shrinking, developments in the complicated world of logistics, etc. There are many hundreds of loading and unloading points, distribution centres and sidings for a breathtaking array of products, producing an almost infinite array of journey permutations. Every month these changes are charted by the likes of the *Freightmaster* organisation.

Just to give an incomplete list of freight traffic in random order, the railways convey or have in recent decades conveyed such things as automobiles, car components, chemicals, industrial minerals such as limestone and china clay, metals, pet food, fertiliser, timber, grain, government stores, ordnance, cider, sugar beet, methanol, propylene, sand, carbon dioxide, hydrogen cyanide, potash, starch, nuclear traffic, light fittings, lime, resin, gypsum, coke, pipes, scrap, steel in various forms, wire, aluminium, bricks, blocks, salt, cement, gravel, roadstone, ballast, sleepers, containers (freightliner/intermodal), liquid petroleum gas, coal, domestic and industrial waste, parcels, mails, newspapers, beer, fish, calcified seaweed, calcium carbonate, petrol, oil, bitumen, concrete, iron ore, pig iron, fly ash, haematite, groceries and a whole lot more.

Some of the traffic carried is seasonal while various commodities are subject to annual fluctuations or simple peaks and troughs in the supply and demand chain. Some loads are short-term contracts, for example the removal of surface coal from a closed pit, or the delivery of stone for local sea defence work, while others may last for years, such as the aggregates or concrete requirements for the building of the Channel Tunnel or the East London site of the 2012 Olympics. Here we examine just a few of these commodities in a little more detail.

Coal has been the primary commodity hauled by rail since the beginning of railway history in the UK. As already mentioned, coal haulage was at one time the only profitable

◀ The Castle Cary to Weymouth line has never been known for its frequency of freight trains but an interesting working that survived into the 1990s was a coal train that served Yeovil Junction. It was a tricky working to photograph in that timings were erratic and the train did not run every day. In March 1992, No 37223 is seen at the Western Region station of Yeovil Pen Mill with a returning train of empty HEA hoppers. *Author*

segment of goods and freight movement on BR. The mgr system in carrying coal from pit head at collieries direct to coal-fired power stations was arguably the epitome of the profitable freight-by-rail business and produced the ultimate efficiencies afforded by rail in the general logistics business. However, there were shocks in store with the government meddling in the businesses of BR's core customers, the NCB, CEGB and BSC.

The statistics were quite remarkable in that before the government reorganised these industries 60 per cent of the *total* annual tonnage of freight hauled by rail, was attributable to the coal sub-sector with 45 per cent pertaining to power station coal. However, between 1988/89 and 1993/94 volume by tonnage and therefore income from the coal source fell by 38 per cent. The slump in the building trade and the closure of Ravenscraig steelworks in 1992 knocked the construction and metals traffic sideways with a 30 per cent reduction, and in a similar five-year period coal traffic fell by 23 per cent. To expect Railfreight to make a profit or positive return on assets in these circumstances was of course naïve.

Reorganisation of our major industries produced a number of agreements, or what at the time were called 'understandings', effectively non-legally binding contracts. The CEGB looked closely at costs and this led to an increase in the amount of coal imported into the UK. During the 1970s about 1 million tonnes of coal was imported per annum but by 1989 this had increased to over 10 million tonnes. Between 1991 and 1994 this swelled to an incredible 16.7 million tonnes per annum, about one-quarter of total domestic production. With North Sea and pipelined gas supplies increasing UK coal production fell from an average of 129 million tonnes per annum in the 1970s to 94 million tonnes in 1991 and a miserly 49 million tonnes in 1994. At the same time coal-fired power stations themselves were under the cosh, with electricity supplies from such installations falling from 60 per cent of the total in 1991 to a mere 42 per cent in 1994, a radical reduction in such a short timescale.

In 1985, despite years of closures, there were still 169 collieries in operation. By 1994, when the industry was sold to private enterprise, only 16 were left! New contracts for this industry in decline were drawn up in 1990. The contracts were riddled with potential complexities relating to performance, inflation, incentives, train movement rate, etc. In a world of falling coal traffic volumes negotiations were difficult but notwithstanding these various provisions the contracts stipulated a minimum annual payment to BR of £175.6 million but with forecast gross revenue of £209 million in 1990/91 falling to £194 million in 1993/94.

Although a quantum leap forward in timescale into a well-established privatised railway, at the time of writing coal-fired power stations receiving their basic fuel supplies by rail were: Longannet, Cockenzie, Drax, Eggborough, Ferrybridge, West Burton, Cottam, Ratcliffe, Rugeley,

Ironbridge, Uskmouth, Aberthaw and Didcot. Collieries or loading points for imported and other coal were: Hunterston, Chalmerston, Killoch, Greenburn, New Cumnock, Ravenstruther, Butterwell, North Blyth, Tyne Dock, Redcar, Hull, Immingham, Welbeck, Thoresby, Daw Mill, Avonmouth, Portbury, Onllwyn and Newport Docks. Industrial and domestic coal has hugely diminished with customers at Rugby, Ketton, Penyffordd, Hope, Scunthorpe and Wilton being served from Hunterston, New Cumnock, Widdrington, Butterwell, Tyne Dock and Immingham.

Other than for carrying coal in block loads one of the great success stories, certainly since the mid-1970s, has been the conveyance of aggregates, a collective expression for stone, gravel and sand. Although it was Prime Minister Harold McMillan who uttered the words 'you've never had it so good' back in 1957, there was another boom in building from the mid-1970s until the late 1980s when, following the coal miners' strike, other negative factors caused a recession and rapidly falling house prices. Until then there was an explosion of building work ranging from housing estates to motorway construction.

Much of this occurred in the south-east, which was music to the ears of the Merehead and Whatley quarry operators in Somerset such as Foster Yeoman (later Aggregate Industries) and Amey Roadstone Corporation (later Hanson), with other firms such as Bardon Aggregates (later also Aggregate Industries) loading in the Frome area. From lean pickings in the early 1970s these companies invested in infrastructure, including conveyors and rapid-loading equipment, capable of loading a 100-tonne wagon in just two minutes. Former branch lines were used for access to the quarries that grew from producing a few tens of thousands of tonnes per annum to over 6 million tonnes.

Over the years the scene changed dramatically with small vacuum-braked four-wheeled tipper wagons giving way to 50-tonne four-wheeled air-braked hopper wagons and later various types of 100-tonne bogie wagons. Changes in motive power already described enabled longer and heavier trains to run with a Class 59 diagrammed daily to operate singly with a gross laden weight of 4,300 tonnes in tow. In 1991, a pair of Class 59s were used in a trial hauling a train of 12,000 tonnes, true USA standards, but the wagon couplings were not man enough for the job leaving the working as nothing more than a trial. At the other end of the stone train network dozens of sites were adapted as aggregate terminals, many on former goods yard and siding sites. Mendip Rail was formed in 1993, bringing together all Somerset quarry rail movements.

There were also developments in Leicestershire with Mountsorrel in particular becoming a focal point for stone and ballast workings, with the Redland company featuring prominently. This traffic was also gradually upgraded on the wagon front with, in 1988, the greatest innovation being the delivery of a 'self-discharge train'. The advantage with this train was its ability to unload itself in any large area without the need for terminal unloading equipment. In addition to commercial customers, for many years Mountsorrel has produced millions of tons of ballast for BR's own use.

Many other ballast quarries, ranging from Meldon in Devon to Penmaenmawr in Conwy were similarly used, but over the years their importance diminished. One of the other great centres for aggregates and other mineral traffic has been the Great Rocks (Tunstead)/Peak Forest (Dove Holes)/Dowlow/Hindlow complexes near Buxton in the Peak District of Derbyshire, where over the years many millions of tons of material have been removed by rail, the most famous load having been limestone to the Northwich area for the old ICI company. In 1997/98, Tunstead despatched 2.3 million tonnes of minerals with the Northwich limestone amounting to nearly 900,000 tonnes.

One special factor at that time was the demand for limestone in connection with the building of a second runway at Manchester Airport. Again, traffic patterns, wagon types and locomotives have all moved with the times over the years notwithstanding peaks and troughs in the industry. The scene is still buoyant and modern in operation except for the survival of some delightful manual semaphore signalling in the Peak Forest and Great Rocks areas.

There has always been a large number of quarry sites involved in producing aggregates for conveyance by rail. As with any aspect of industry, quarries that were once prolific contributors to the railfreight industry are no longer operational but at the time of writing aggregates and construction materials carried by rail originate at Rylestone, Dowlow, Tunstead, Dove Holes, Mountsorrel, Stud Farm, Bardon Hill, Croft, Marks Tey, Ipswich, Cliffe, Angerstein Wharf, Wool, Whatley, Merehead, Moreton-on-Lugg, Neath, Avonmouth and Machen.

Something in the region of 70 customer terminals nationwide are served from these originating points; too many to detail here. Many of these were established with the aid of a Section 8 Grant. Most are aligned with specific companies including Mendip Rail, Lafarge, Tarmac, Brett, RMC, BLI, Marcon and Aggregate Industries and again, over time, many other companies have come and gone. The corporate world is extremely volatile and it is difficult for the layman to keep up with events 'in the City of London'. For example, English China Clays owned quarries but they demerged this sector of the business, which became Camas. Camas subsequently merged with Bardon Aggregates, the conglomerate becoming Aggregate Industries.

In the late 1980s aggregates moved by rail peaked at about 18 million tonnes and after the recession of the 1989–93 period this had shrunk to just 11 million tonnes. Traffic bottomed out at 9 million tonnes in 1996/97 increasing to some 11 million tonnes in 1997/98. After privatisation EWS managed to grow the traffic to over 20 million tonnes per annum, a significant achievement. In the early part of the 21st century some former EWS flows were subsequently taken over by Freightliner Heavy Haul and as contracts come up for renewal and tender forms are issued there will no doubt continue to be a perpetual roundabout of freight operators gaining and losing traffic within the same financial year.

A more recent development has been the creation of 'virtual quarries' where mountains of aggregates are unloaded from ships or by multiple trainloads and stockpiled so that customer peaks can be satisfied and the need to run special trains outside of a regular scheduled service pattern is eliminated. It has also enabled a large number of smaller quarries from Meldon to Shap to be closed, at least in terms of appearing on the railway map.

Construction material by way of cement and concrete has again radically changed over the years, and with few exceptions the present cement works and terminals 'map' bears little resemblance to that of the 1948 to 1997 BR years. For decades cement was conveyed in the distinctive 'Presflo' four-wheeled wagons. They were carted around the system in wagonloads to wherever there happened to be a building project. However, there were also block loads and Class 33 fans will recall pictures from the 1960s with pairs of 'Cromptons' hauling the long-distance, 450-mile Cliffe to Uddington train of vacuum-braked 'Cemflo' wagons. Gradually, the industry procured private owner wagons replacing the largely BR-owned 'Presflos'.

In the mid-1970s there were over 70 cement terminals but as with other commodities there was considerable rationalisation as central distribution points became more cost-effective. The industry was to a considerable degree impacted by the reduction in wagonload services already discussed, but the cost benefit analysis of rail versus road was swinging in the direction of the latter. Again, the corporate world changed the face of the industry with Tunnel Cement, Ribblesdale Cement, Ketton Cement and Castle Cement all becoming part of the RTZ empire. By the end of the 1980s all the old vacuum-braked cement wagons had gone; the 'Presflo' was dead.

Cement by rail was in seemingly terminal decline as flow after flow was lost to road. The famous Blue Circle cement company became part of Lafarge in 2001. However, it was the advent of privatisation that saved certain cement-by-rail traffic flows and eventually both EWS and Freightliner signed contracts with cement-producing companies with Lafarge aiming to send 1 million tonnes of cement by rail each year. Cement and concrete products now originate from Oxwellmains, Clitheroe, Hope, Tunstead, Heck and Ketton. Most of the output travels to Moorswater, Westbury, Theale, St Pancras, Bow, West Thurrock, Biggleswade, Walsall, Weaste, Dewsbury, Hunslet, Uddington, Seaham, Mossend, Aberdeen and Inverness, but again the customers and routes vary almost monthly and further changes may have occurred recently.

The conveyance of petroleum and oil by rail goes back to a period that substantially pre-dated British Railways. However, over the past 40 years the story has been one of significant decline as tonnages by rail have plummeted. From the early 1960s through to the early 1970s, prior to the construction of a comprehensive pipeline network, the UK had a growing love affair with the motor car and the demand for petrol and in more rural parts a demand for domestic heating oil, resulted in a large number of regional terminals being built.

Local distribution from these terminals was of course by road tanker. The industry was one of the first to heavily invest in private owner wagons and in the early and mid-1960s the oil company's name or logo was emblazoned on the sides of the tank wagons. The move from vacuum- to air-braked wagons was an early progression, starting in the mid-1960s. In fact, having procured at first 45-tonne and then 51-tonne air-braked wagons the industry was one of the first to order and operate large bogie tankers grossing at 102 tonnes for use on their large volume traffic flows. Sector rail traffic peaked at a whopping 20 million tonnes per annum in the early 1970s, but there followed an inextricable decline averaging 650,000 tonnes per annum for some 20 years, reducing to just 7 million tonnes by the time privatisation was being considered, and stabilising at 7.4 million tonnes in 1999.

Modern logistics, where sophisticated costing systems determine the most cost-effective way of distributing each and every product, have had an impact. It seems that the elimination of large numbers of essentially local depots, which were effectively decentralised storage tanks, and their replacement by central distribution centres has been the preferred option. Even where small oil terminals were purpose built, with a single commodity function, they became vulnerable as road distribution from a decreasing number of refineries became more attractive in terms of cost and flexibility.

In addition to road transport competition the advances made in pipeline technology resulted in a matrix of pipelines spreading throughout the country. Pipelines were expensive to build but the capital outlay was repaid in reliability of delivery terms, affording the optimum control of flows. Long-term cost benefit analysis showed a positive return over the cost of overland transportation by road or rail, and any likelihood of industrial disputes were removed at a stroke. Another reason for a decline in Petroleum Sector traffic was a reduction in demand for oil-based products, due to the closure of oil-fired power stations and other installations, especially when North Sea gas came on tap in ever-increasing volumes. The decline and eventual withdrawal of wagonload freight adversely impacted the sector, except for heavy oils and bitumen that was not easily piped.

In national terms the largest installation for transporting petroleum products by rail is Lindsey, near Immingham. In the 1960s, Fawley in Hampshire was a major rail centre for rail tanker traffic but now it is barely a shadow compared with its heyday, with only a handful of trains per week and only 5 per cent of its total production being conveyed by rail. Traditionally, some of the major loading points for Petroleum Sector trains were Robeston, Waterston and Herbrandston terminals in the Milford Haven area, Llandarcy in South Wales, Thames Haven, Shell Haven and Coryton on the Thames estuary, Grain in Kent, Lindsey and Humber refineries near Immingham, Stanlow and Ellesmere Port in the North West, Port Clarence in the North East, in the Grangemouth area in the Scottish lowlands and many, many others.

By 1990, Ellesmere Port had closed (to bitumen traffic) and by 1998 only Robeston survived for rail traffic in south-

▶ It may make perhaps a refreshing change in a railway book for an author to admit that he has absolutely no idea about the identity of a particular train. Such was the case at Kensington Olympia in August 1994 when Network SouthEast No 47711 passed by heading towards Willesden with a pair of BG vans with their windows coated. Were they barrier vehicles, or full of gold bullion? Whatever its identity, this was an interesting non-passenger working and has therefore been included in this volume. *Author*

west Wales, Waterston having closed in 1997 (albeit with some residual traffic until 1999). In petrol/oil by rail terms Llandarcy closed in 1999, the large Stanlow loading point operated by Shell succumbed to pipelines in 1998, and Shell Haven also closed in 1999. An unusual loss was the closure of the customer depot at Heathfield in Devon, on the old Moretonhampstead branch line from Newton Abbot, which lost out to coastal shipping that took the oil by coastal tanker from Milford Haven to Plymouth. In addition to refinery closures some classic loads were lost such as the latterly Class 60-hauled Immingham to Langley 2,750-tonne trains containing aviation fuel for Heathrow Airport, which ended in 2003.

Perhaps the greatest loss, for the reasons described in the preceding paragraphs, has been the closure of unloading terminals at smaller regional distribution centres. Scores of these once-viable installations are now abandoned and some are derelict. Some had a reasonable trainload delivered daily while others received only a couple of tankers per week. Although the victims of progress it is modern history that their closure has created. On the positive side petrochemicals are still delivered by rail, mainly in large block loads, but with a few exceptions to mainly railway diesel depots! At the time of writing petrochemicals are despatched from Fawley, Robeston, Immingham, Port Clarence, Harwich and Grangemouth to about 25 locations, some of them very 'part-time'.

One of the most complicated stories concerns what was latterly known as trainload metals. For years and in grossly simplified terms trains worked around a corridor from Ravenscraig in Scotland via Shotton (Dee Marsh) to South Wales. Steel trains also operated to and from major installations in the Teesside, Scunthorpe, Consett, Corby and Sheerness areas to lesser terminals nationwide. The actual method of steel processing heavily influenced the industry and the movement of raw materials and both finished and part or unfinished products resulting in much variety. In many instances one steel plant would produce steel in one form and it would then be transported to another site for finishing.

Steel and other metal products were wide-ranging from hot and cold coil, to slabs, bars, billets, plate, strip, rods, tinplate, rail lengths, wire, pipes, haematite, aluminium and scrap metal. For decades the raw material of iron ore was sourced within the UK but by 1967 and the subsequent creation of the British Steel Corporation, described in a previous chapter, domestic ores were no longer used because they were more expensive than imported materials. Huge volumes of iron ore were transported to blast furnaces from the likes of Bidston Dock, Newport Docks, Immingham, Redcar, Tyne Dock and Hunterston in Scotland.

In the early days of BR there were a large number of iron and steel works, mostly but not entirely located in the Midlands and the north of the country. Many of these had been in operation since the Industrial Revolution when the UK was one of the greatest manufacturing countries in the world. Gradually, during the post-war years leading up to Nationalisation, the rest of the world had the opportunity of re-tooling and modernising plant and within a few decades the words 'developing nations' became part of the vocabulary. Wages were cheap, raw materials were readily available, there were no conditions of employment and no trade unions, and before we knew it we were importing not only raw material but finished steel products into the country.

These imports were cheaper than certain UK products despite the cost of shipping them halfway around the world. This resulted in widespread company failures and plant closures. The obvious consequence of these closures was the simultaneous closure of the associated railheads, yards and sidings, with a knock-on reduction in the annual tonnage-by-rail statistics. Some closures were significant in social and local economic terms such as Workington in 2006, bringing to an end nearly 130 years of steel production at the plant. Yet again there were numerous corporate changes including a period of nationalisation before the industry was privatised again.

The specification of a multitude of steel-carrying wagon types improved and as with other trainloads their brakes, suspension, bearings, capacity and speed improved. Many of the Metals Sector steel trains have always been heavy, often necessitating double heading. The motive power scene developed over the years, changing from elderly steam engines to Class 9F 2-10-0 freight engines, progressing to modern diesel traction. At one stage in the late 1970s, triple-headed Class 37s were used on iron ore trains in South Wales between Port Talbot and Llanwern, to be replaced by pairs of 3,250hp Class 56s. For years, steel coil trains required double-headed Class 37 motive power and in the 1990s specially ballasted and re-engined Class 37/9s were used, prior to the arrival of the Class 60 fleet.

After many years of decline a combination of steel industry rationalisation and railway privatisation saw traffic levels increase from 9.8 million tonnes in 1993/94 to 14.2 million tons in 1997/98. Part of the increase was imported iron ore, which was conveyed in 3,000-tonne trains and in 1997/98 totalled 5 million tonnes per annum. With a recession again affecting the industry during the 2008–11 period it remains to be seen how metals traffic will hold up, but there is no doubt that steel products will continue to be conveyed by rail for a considerable time.

The Freightliner business in terms of containers and intermodal traffic has had a very mixed story since its inception. In the early days of British Railways containers were, visually, small almost square boxes tethered to short wheelbase four-wheeled vacuum-braked flat wagons that were delivered to goods yards, lifted by cranes and then whisked off normally by BR road vehicles to waiting customers. Other than for the container concept and using a road/rail combination those meagre beginnings bear little resemblance to the modern metal containers in use today, which are not only used domestically but internationally, being stacked on vast ocean-going vessels often weighing over 100,000 tonnes. These ships literally travel the world with containers being handled in highly mechanised yards prior to being transported to waiting customers.

The container has a vast number of advantages over older shipping methods. They are secure, robust, high capacity, easily handled and capable of holding almost any commodity. In 2007, when the container ship *Napoli* came to grief and containers were washed up on the Devon coast and looting took place, it was fascinating to see a complete miscellany of merchandise emerging from various containers, including car parts, boxes of shampoo, personal possessions from a house move, and even BMW motorcycles.

As already mentioned, Freightliner trains as we now know them, started to operate in 1965. It was a revelation when modern long-wheelbase wagons started to operate at 75mph. With methods of international shipping changing radically at the expense of old traditional docks, with their lines of cranes and an inefficient manpower-heavy operation, it was inevitable that before long a Freightliner network would begin to appear on brand-new purpose-built sites. Beeching had talked about a form of containerisation for purely domestic freight, referring to them as 'Liner' trains, but he could not have envisaged worldwide containerisation.

The problem with a purely domestic operation was the age-old one of short distances and costly double handling at the shipping and receiving terminals. However, where the operation was part of a multi thousand-mile journey the overall economics became viable. Despite the growth in traffic, particularly at Southampton and Felixstowe, the mid- to late 1980s and early 1990s were unkind to Freightliner

and poor loadings suggested that perhaps the business had outgrown itself, and several depots closed. Despite this retraction there were still well over 100 Freightliner trains running every day in the UK and just to give scale to the operation, in 1998 Felixstowe handled over 200,000 'boxes' and Felixstowe and Southampton together had 25 train arrivals and 25 departures every weekday. The name 'Freightliner' became the franchised brand name for the deep-sea container network.

In recent years and especially since the privatisation of the railways, terminals have come and gone while at some locations new replacement terminals have been constructed. For example, at Cardiff the original Pengam installation was replaced by a new container handling depot at Wentloog. At the time of writing the total Freightliner map serves installations at Southampton Maritime and Millbrook, Wentloog, Thamesport (Grain), Ripple Lane, Tilbury, Felixstowe (north and south), Daventry, Lawley Street, Hams Hall and Birch Coppice (the last three in the greater Birmingham area), Basford Hall (Crewe), Garston and Ditton (both on Merseyside), Trafford Park (Manchester), Leeds, Doncaster, Wilton (Cleveland) and Coatbridge in Scotland. The theory is that any permutation of container traffic between any of these locations can run, but the only place where actual marshalling takes place is at Crewe.

If the Intermodal network is added to the overall container scene, even though such traffic is separately identified and run by a variety of operators including DB Schenker and GBRf, then terminals at Southampton (Western Docks), Dollands Moor (Channel Tunnel), Wembley Yard, Ipswich, Burton upon Trent, Wakefield, Selby, Tees Dock, Mossend, Grangemouth, Aberdeen and Inverness can be added to the location map, in addition the aforementioned Thamesport, Tilbury, Felixstowe, Daventry, Hams Hall, Birch Coppice, Trafford Park, Doncaster and Coatbridge.

▶ This single-track spur is the lead into Bedford station from the Bletchley and Bedford St John's direction on what was once a spur off a long cross-country line from Oxford to Cambridge. Class 56 No 56056 is hauling empty rubbish containers from Forders Sidings at Stewartby, where tons of London's rubbish is dumped in pits left over from old brickworks excavations. The locomotive will run round its train at Bedford Midland station before heading back to Hendon. *Author*

The future for the container businesses looks strong and the use of special wagons and boxes with low decks allowing larger containers to be carried, while remaining within the UK loading gauge, in addition to 'swapbody' containers, has had benefits. The loading gauge north from Southampton to the Midlands has recently been increased with further plans to convert the alternative diversionary route via Romsey and Andover. Also, with shipping volumes slowly increasing after a serious recession and with DB Schenker using its acquisitions of European freight companies to increase their Channel Tunnel freight business, both the Freightliner and Intermodal businesses should prosper.

On the automotive front, cars and components are still moved about the country in some volume. Pictures of old Rootes Group Hillman Imps being transferred on open wagons now seem a millennium away. The Jaguars, Fords, Hondas and BMWs of this world still move freight by rail. French car manufacturers have been using Corby as a UK distribution point. Some traffic uses the Channel Tunnel but other terminals are located at Purfleet, Dagenham, Southampton, Bridgend, Portbury (Avonmouth), South Marston (Swindon), Oxford, Castle Bromwich, Halewood, Garston, Tyne Dock and Mossend, although in the past, other locations have been used as far apart as Newhaven in East Sussex and Bathgate in Scotland.

Some flows are quite remarkable, such as a Ford train from Valencia in Spain to Dagenham. This flow was run by Transfesa but with DB Schenker taking over both Transfesa and EWS it would appear that the Ford company could be tied to DB for some time. For decades completed cars were conveyed in special 'Cartic' wagons but the top deck of cars were open, with obvious risks from vandals, theft or large hailstones. During the last decade or two modern wagons have mostly been completely enclosed. The advent of four-wheel-drive people-carrying 'Chelsea Tractors' has caused problems because their extra height has resulted in single-deck loads. One bit of good news for the new privatised freight operators was the introduction in 1999 of new car registration letters twice a year, thereby avoiding what had been an acute annual peak in traffic as large volumes of new cars were demanded for the July/August period.

Another couple of traffic flows worthy of special mention are Ministry of Defence loads and nuclear waste trains. In the case of the former it is strategically important to retain a UK rail network to a reasonable number of military installations, even though the number has fallen over the years. A wide range of commodities from military vehicles to munitions and stores are moved by rail. MoD sites include Marchwood, Ludgershall, Hoo Junction, Cardiff (Wentloog), Haverfordwest, Kineton, Bicester, Shoeburyness, Donnington, Eastriggs and Longtown, with traffic hubs being Eastleigh, Wembley, Arpley (Warrington) and Carlisle. There are a handful of sites where there is very occasional MoD traffic and some have had a 'stop/go' history such as Redmire, Warminster, Wool, Caerwent and East Dereham.

Most of the traffic is integrated within the Enterprise network between hubs and is tripped to MoD depots. Nuclear traffic is, nowadays, carried in dedicated trainloads such is the sensitivity of their movements by rail. Rather unkindly some enthusiasts have dubbed these trains as 'the bomb'. The trains convey spent nuclear fuel in special and immensely strong crash-proof containers. All of this traffic is conveyed from nuclear power stations or their respective railheads to Sellafield reprocessing plant in Cumbria. These

◄ When the Class 60s started to be delivered a large number of teething problems took a considerable time to resolve and many months elapsed before BR were prepared to take them into stock. Problems included cylinder heads, axle box suspension units and microprocessor faults, with each new locomotive averaging 100 faults detected. Inevitably they settled down and faults were slowly rectified. Powering up the GW route to Birmingham at Fenny Compton in September 1992 is Coal Sector 'Tug' No 60067 with Theale to Lindsey bogie tanks. It is interesting to note that the main line has upper quadrant semaphore signals but the siding leading to the MoD depot at Kineton on the old Stratford-upon-Avon & Midland Junction Railway alignment is controlled by lower quadrant examples. *Author*

originating power stations are Hinkley Point, Oldbury, Dungeness, Bradwell, Sizewell, Wylfa, Seaton-on-Tees, Heysham, Torness and Hunterston.

In 1998, British Nuclear Fuels decided they should have control over all of their nuclear transport operations by creating a subsidiary company called Direct Rail Services, or DRS. The DRS company employed older first-generation ex-BR main line diesel locomotives repainted in their own novel livery, although in later years, modern locomotive acquisitions have been made. The company later branched out into the general railfreight business and has since won a number of contracts.

There are of course many other traffic flows, already listed and too numerous to detail. About 1 million tons of china clay per annum is transported by rail in the West Country although volumes are in decline. There are large volumes of gypsum and a variety of chemicals moved around the rail network and the movement by rail of domestic and industrial waste compacted in containers is burgeoning. Often overlooked is the movement of what is known as infrastructure services, which includes all of what was once known as BR departmental and civil engineers traffic, ranging from track and ballast to sleepers and spoil, as well as track machinery and contractors' equipment. This traffic accounts for a massive 15 per cent of DBS business. Back in 1999, this traffic still used 2,000 vacuum-braked wagons out of the 6,000 employed on such duties, the last of a rapidly dying breed. Enterprise freight continues to handle all manner of commodities.

In preparing this book it became evident that the evolution that has occurred since British Railways was formed over 60 years ago has been remarkable. Looking at the photographs contained herein, the sight of an ancient, 41-ton Caledonian Railway 0-6-0 Drummond 'standard goods' of 1883 manufacture clanking along with just two goods wagons and a brake van in 1959, and a 129-tonne 3,690hp North American 'PowerHaul' General Electric Class 70 Co-Co high-tech computer-controlled diesel-electric hauling 30 high-capacity air-braked bogie coal wagons in 2010 is in fact beyond comparison!

Most major changes have been shown in this volume whether they be locomotives, infrastructure, payloads or train workings. Although privatisation has had many critics and in parts the transition from BR days has been retrograde, overall, goods and freight traffic has been a success story in terms of profitability, at the expense of total tonnage carried by rail. The freight industry has become more efficient, genuine competition is present in the market, movement by rail is now taken seriously and there is no doubt that inward investment has been forthcoming. Most British patriots no doubt lament that many UK companies have been taken over by 'foreign' firms such as English China Clays becoming part of the French Imerys company, Blue Circle Cement becoming part of the French Lafarge concern, 'Mini' cars are being built by the German BMW company, our steel

industry being substantially in the hands of Tata, an Indian corporation, American General Motors and General Electric locomotives powering many of our freight trains, which often comprise French-built wagons, a significant part of all UK freight being moved by the German DB Schenker company, and so on. The fact is, like it or not, we are now part of a competitive global economy where often it is the financial 'bottom line' that drives all forms of industry. We are all, to some degree, resistant to change and we seem to wallow in nostalgia, where nothing is as good as it once was.

There is no doubt that the world of railfreight has changed out of all recognition since Nationalisation in 1948. There is little doubt that Dr Beeching's findings in the Reshaping Report of 1963 clearly identified loss-making goods and freight traffic on BR, and many of his recommendations have stood the test of time. The many twists and turns within the BR organisation and the degree of government interference have been remarkable, as has the rise and fall of many of our great industries. There were great hopes in the mid-1990s when the proactive management of EWS started to win contracts that returned freight loads to the railways.

There have been successes and failures even in this privatised world and some small freight operators have failed. However, with DB Schenker, Freightliner, GB Railfreight, Direct Rail Services and Colas all competing for traffic there is always going to be breaking news in the UK railfreight market. Some of our great industries continue to decline and such changes will directly impact the railways, such as a reducing reliance on fossil fuels, but one merely has to observe the southbound traffic at the Birmingham end of the M6 motorway on any morning of the week to realise that there is plenty of potential out there to increase the railways' 11.5 per cent share of the overland goods market in the UK.

With the price of diesel fuel escalating there could well be a golden opportunity for the railways. The UK motorway system is woefully inadequate and while motorists will lament this short-sighted lack of investment by government, it could transpire that lorry journey times become so long, compounded at times by the M25 becoming permanently gridlocked, that rail transportation becomes attractive to more companies, notwithstanding the recent withdrawal of development grants for rail connection. Also, there is no reason why Channel Tunnel freight traffic should not increase and as mentioned previously, in recent months DB Schenker has been in discussion with the Russians about the possibility of developing through freight workings from Europe to China!

From the contemporary enthusiasts' perspective freight will end up being the main focal point of interest on our railways with just about every passenger train in the land being unit based and without that all-important ingredient of a locomotive. It has been a pleasure to share the remarkable *The Rise and Fall of British Railways: Goods & Freight* story with you, and I hope you have enjoyed the journey.

◄ There seems to be Class 20 infestation at Cosford on 30 January 1990, despite Class 58s working a number of Ironbridge Power Station merry-go-round trains at the time. Heading empties towards Wolverhampton on the left are Nos 20117 and 20006, while Nos 20143 and 20134 are being held in the down loop with loads for Ironbridge. Semaphore signalling prevailed adding to the nostalgia of the scene. *Author*

◄ Another length of track where it is almost impossible to photograph locomotive-hauled trains is the line down to the Littlehampton terminus in West Sussex, other than for the very occasional railway enthusiast Chartex special. Delivering a little something for the weekend in terms of spoil wagons, diggers and cranes, which is tantamount to freight, is No 33118 that had worked down from Three Bridges, on 16 January 1993. *Author*

◄ Although the British Steel Corporation had brought 14 privately owned companies under a single Nationalised umbrella, over the years there was massive rationalisation and the total workforce more than halved. Prime Minister Mrs Thatcher privatised British Steel in 1988 and in 1999 it was taken over by the Dutch Corus group. Corus was in turn acquired by the Indian Tata Steel Company in 2007. In spite of these changes the steel trains continued to run, as depicted in this scene at Gloucester on 31 December 1990 with Nos 37069 and 37109 working north with a train from Llanwern. *Author*

◄ Winter lighting at Eastleigh illuminates a busy scene with Class 73/0 No 73005 *Mid-hants Watercress Line* in the foreground, while in the background is red-liveried No 47569 *The Gloucestershire Regiment* on vans, and Nos 47381 and 47294 on the Portfield to Ripple Lane empty tanks. Animation is provided by the driver climbing into the cab of No 47381. *Author*

▼ It was a tough job finding photographs of 'Deltic' locomotives on freight trains but in the author's own collection was this very unusual shot of what could be called an exhibition train. On 4/5 May 1991 an open day was held at Wimbledon depot and Yeoman Class 59 No 59003 was entrusted with moving some exhibits from Old Oak Common, which included Class 55s Nos D9016 *Gordon Highlander* and D9000 *Royal Scots Grey* and two Yeoman 100-tonne bogie wagons. The location is of course Clapham Junction, still the busiest station on the UK rail network. *Author*

▲ Well off the beaten track is this photograph taken in the depths of the railway network at Whatley Quarry in Somerset in May 1992. On the right is the wagon repair and maintenance shop while outside is a rich variety of mostly bogie wagons. Arriving through a swirl of exhaust is No 56056 with a long train of empties. Following the success that Foster Yeoman had enjoyed with the GM Class 59s ARC also ordered a quartet of locomotives from the same source in 1990. *Author*

▼ As a result of the mass closures of Nottinghamshire collieries in the late 1980s and early 1990s, the use of UK domestic coal at Didcot Power Station gradually dwindled. Instead, imported coal was used to fire the boilers, most of this being landed at Newport in South Wales or at Avonmouth. In May 1992 the old order is seen with No 58043 storming past the decaying remains of Aynho station, which closed in December 1964. Traditionally this was the point where the boundary between the Western and London Midland Regions was located but this was later moved to just south of Fenny Compton. *Author*

▲ When photographed in September 1993 it was debatable whether the imported Class 59 or the old Great Western Railway seat was the anachronism at Bradford-on-Avon station. Rumbling between the ancient mid-Victorian-age platforms is No 59001 with a Merehead to Hallen Marsh stone train. The route is shared with Cardiff to Portsmouth and Bristol to Weymouth services, but freight traffic is minimal. *Author*

▼ This wonderful industrial landscape featuring Harworth Colliery is full of interest. Coal had been mined in the area for 90 years but Harworth is presently mothballed rather than officially closed, following geological problems at the main coal seam. The branch line serving the complex is presently 'disused' rather than closed and lifted. In happier times, 'Grid' No 56023 leaves the colliery with loaded mgr wagons, on 26 March 1990. *Gavin Morrison*

▲ In its stunning Loadhaul livery 'Grid' Class 56 No 56090 joins the main line at Whitley Bridge with a long rake of empty HAA wagons comprising train 6G09, on 29 March 1997, as it makes its way back to Immingham Coal Import Terminal. In previous years it would have been conveying British-mined coal. In the left background is the vast Eggborough coal-powered power station where the train would have been unloaded while it was still on the move. *Anthony Guppy*

▼ During 1990, the ac electric Class 90 locomotives that had mainly been associated with the West Coast Main Line took over a number of Freightliner and other air-braked freights on the old Great Eastern Railway main line in East London and southern East Anglia. These partly displaced the number of Class 86s on such routes. Starting its ascent of Barking flyover with train 6M37 from Dagenham on 2 March 1992, is No 90132. A London Transport Underground train can be seen on the left. *Anthony Guppy*

TO PRIVATISATION AND BEYOND

▲ The sectorisation of BR during the late 1980s and the creation of various 'shadow' business sectors in the 1990s produced seemingly perpetual change as privatisation loomed. Class 60s continued to be delivered but by the end of the decade the entire freight motive power scene was to change as old British-built locomotives were pensioned off. When photographed in July 1999 there would be little time to savour sights such as this because the Class 66 takeover was about to start. No 37676 passes small boats bobbing on the high tide at Golant in Cornwall with CDA wagons full of china clay destined for Carne Point, Fowey. This locomotive was still working hard for West Coast Railways in 2011. *Author*

▼ It is remarkable (some may say refreshing) that despite Dr Beeching's 1963 findings that short-distance goods trains, wagonload freight and 'tripping' to and from customer locations were heavy loss makers, clearly indicating that the only way forward for freight was point to point block loads, 48 years later trains such as this still operate. Passing Southampton on 18 March 2011 is DB Schenker Class 66 No 66076, still in EWS livery, with 6V38, a very short MoD train from Marchwood to Didcot comprising just two vans containing loads for Longtown, Barry and Bicester. *Author*

◄ The opening of the Channel Tunnel in 1994 had a significant impact on the European travel scene as Eurostars sped their way through the British countryside between London Waterloo and either Paris or Brussels. However, for many the primary benefit was the introduction of 'Le Shuttle' (now 'Eurotunnel Shuttle') whereby road vehicles ranging from small cars to articulated lorries could cross the English Channel from Folkestone to Coquelles in half an hour, whatever the weather, however stormy the seas, and whether or not French fishermen were on strike! The 25kV Eurotunnel Class 9 locomotives were built by Brush and are of a Bo-Bo-Bo triple-bogie design. Although such trains could not travel on BR due to their loading gauge restrictions, they evolved in the BR era. This train is on the Folkestone loop in August 1995. *Author*

▼ It is no secret that for many years since the opening of the Channel Tunnel general freight volumes have been disappointing, at least compared with original forecasts of 35 freights per day. To handle Channel Tunnel freight traffic Class 92 dual-voltage locomotives were ordered from Brush. The locomotives were delivered late and in operation they interfered with track circuiting and signalling. The managing director of Railfreight Distribution described them as 'the most complicated locomotives known to mankind'. The bugs were eventually ironed out and the class became widely used. No 92012 in EWS/DB ownership passes Winnick Junction with 4M67 10.22 Mossend to Hams Hall intermodal on 10 May 2010. *Author*

▲ Over the years one of the national epicentres for freight traffic has been the delightful location of Barnetby in north Lincolnshire. Traffic appears from four directions, in 2011 there were still forests of semaphore signals and there are several trains per hour, whether it be single-car DMUs or 2,000-tonne freights. An overbridge gives a great view of proceedings, such as this scene from 24 September 2009 with, on the right, Freightliner Class 66 No 66581 on 6Z35 Drax to Immingham empties passing EWS No 66117 with up coal train 6C75, while No 66158 on more coal is looped on the left, all seen through a 300mm Nikkor lens on Fuji 200 asa film. *Author*

▼ In BR days there always seemed to be a locomotive that in some respect was a 'one-off' roaming the network and to secure a photograph was always satisfying. In April 1990 such a machine was No 50019 *Ramillies* that was working out of Plymouth Laira on civil engineers' trains, having earlier been returned to blue livery. With the town of Liskeard as a backdrop and with Liskeard station just visible top left the 'Hoover' is seen crossing Bolitho Viaduct with old vacuum-braked wagons full of used ballast. The class would be sorely missed, especially the sound of the 16-cylinder English Electric engine. *Author*

◀ The new Railfreight livery tended to suit Class 26s and in a flattering way gave the impression that the locomotives were much younger than they were. On 16 August 1992, No 26041 is seen on a civil engineer's ballast train at Blackford in Perthshire, a few miles on the Stirling side of Gleneagles and the summit of the line. *John Chalcraft/Rail Photoprints*

◀ Few photographs seem to be published of Fife, north of the Firth of Forth in the Scottish lowlands. In this attractive scene at Lochgelly, Nos 20137 and 20198 are seen heading an air-braked freight from Mossend to its initial destination of Thornton Junction, on 30 May 1990. Many of the loads would be tripped to customers from Thornton Junction, one of the costlier elements of running the train. *John Chalcraft/ Rail Photoprints*

◀ The average enthusiast had much to digest in the pre-privatisation years. Railfreight introduced a revised livery in 1988 and new sectors within the Railfreight umbrella appeared, including Trainload Construction, Coal, Metals, Petroleum, Distribution and General, each with a unique decal that was applied to the bodysides of that sector's locomotives. In this view, the bold Petroleum Sector decal is illustrated as No 37892 prepares to leave Micheldever, north of Winchester, with empty bogie tanks for Ripple Lane. *Author*

▶ By the late 1980s the Parcels Sector was a financial disaster. Already reduced to just Red Star and Royal Mail letters the sector was re-branded as 'Rail Express Systems' and a new red livery was applied with blue blocks and dashes on the bodysides, that nobody understood. The sector continued in their failure to meet targets even though the Post Office had made significant investments at their end of the business. Eventually, Red Star was disposed of via a management buyout for a small sum in 1995 and EWS acquired RES in 1997. A glowing RES-liveried No 47738 *Bristol Barton Hill* and matching vans stands at Reading in September 1995. *Author*

▶ One of the more attractive but now freight-only lines is from Saltburn West Junction, a few miles east of Middlesbrough, to Boulby-Cleveland Potash, on what was once the old coastal route to Whitby and Scarborough. Running along the cliff tops at Hunt Cliff near Brotton with the 12.47 Tees Dock to Boulby potash empties, is EWS-liveried No 56113, on 21 September 2001. *John Chalcraft/ Rail Photoprints*

▶ Illustrated here is a most unusual operation whereby a BR Speedlink freight started its journey on a preserved railway line. Fitzgerald Lighting loaded its light fittings and equipment into VGA vans at sidings on the outskirts of Bodmin. The BR wagons were then tripped down to Bodmin Parkway where they were collected by a BR and later EWS locomotive. In this June 1997 view the Bodmin & Wenford Railway's Class 20 No 20166 *River Fowey* has arrived at the exchange siding stop blocks and EWS No 37521 is about to pick up the four wagons. This is another operation that has now ceased. *Author*

▶ Although in many respects the performance of Classes 59, 66, 67 and 70 must be admired, one of the pleasures of the post-BR decades has been observing British-built diesels in action, some of which date back over half a century. Four ageing Class 20s were employed on a modern rolling stock movement from Derby to Old Dalby test track on 14 May 2010. Passing Stenson Junction in fine form are Nos 20905 and 20901 leading with Nos 20142 and 20189 tailing, barrier vehicles being used between locomotives and stock. *Author*

◀ Direct Rail Services has made good use of redundant Class 37s that have been acquired from various sources. In March 2011 they purchased the remainder of the EWS (now DB Schenker) Class 37 fleet of 13 locomotives, including several non-runners for spares. Back in August 2007, DRS Nos 37605 and 37606 were used to top and tail a track-recording train, seen passing Goring-by-Sea in West Sussex. *Author*

◀ As a short-term expedient to supply more reliable motive power to its Freightliner customer, Porterbrook Leasing contracted to re-engine a dozen Class 47s with 12-cylinder General Motor prime movers, Brush alternators and new control equipment, the locomotives becoming Class 57s. In June 2004, No 57012 *Freightliner Envoy* was performing the duties it was designed for as it approached Eastleigh with an up container train. Freightliner later procured additional Class 66s and their Class 57s were no longer required, but they had served a stop-gap purpose. *Author*

▲ Since the Class 59s were introduced they have received several liveries but notwithstanding the emergence of Mendip Rail in 1993 No 59005 *Kenneth J Painter* was still in Yeoman livery at Reading in May 2005 as it headed train 7C77, Acton to Merehead empties. The train comprised JNA bogie wagons and it would travel via Reading West and take to the Berks & Hants line at Southcote Junction. Notice the third rail in the bay platform, used by South West Trains EMUs on services to Waterloo. *Author*

▼ An unusual sight on the 6V18 Hither Green to Whatley Quarry on Friday 5 November 2004 was double-headed Class 59/1s Nos 59104 *Village of Great Elm* and 59103 *Village of Mells* in Hanson livery, seen passing Kensington Olympia. No 59103 had received accident damage, note the badly bent handrail and scraped cabside, and this could have been the reason for the movement. It is hard to believe that over a quarter of a century has passed since the first Class 59s arrived in the UK. *Author*

◀ Although the Class 67s arrived on these shores during the 1999/2000 period and were never part of the 'pure' BR scene, an illustration to complete the post-privatisation freight scene is justified. Although mainly used on passenger trains, Chartex specials and even the Royal Train, these Alstom Spanish-built 3,200hp Bo-Bo locomotives regularly work freights, such as No 67027 seen speeding through Doncaster on the up fast line in June 2005. *Author*

◀ There is still plenty of freight in the North East of the UK focussed in the general environs of Tees and Tyne Yards. Passing Middlesbrough signalbox with steel flats bound for Redcar is EWS Class 66 No 66229. Due to the recession of the 2008–11 period, large numbers of Class 66s were moved to mainland Europe by DB Schenker who are pan-European operators. The German company gained a valuable asset in the shape of the EWS Class 66 fleet when they acquired that company. *Author*

◀ Under the shadow business arrangements and the creation of Loadhaul, Mainline and Transrail, another set of new liveries emerged but their lifespan was comparatively short as privatisation took hold. Significant procurements also took place including not only large numbers of General Motors Class 66 variants but also the first locomotives to operate in the UK from the US General Electric stable. These 3,650hp 'PowerHaul' machines acquired for Freightliner were impressive but some say aesthetically displeasing, albeit with some brutal appeal. Gradually their travels widened and on 3 August 2011 No 70007 was photographed approaching Eastleigh with train 4V52, 10.52 Southampton Maritime to Wentloog. *Author*

▲ Although suburban electrification from Liverpool Street had slowly but surely progressed eastward from the Capital over the decades it was the late 1980s when electrification reached Manningtree, Ipswich and later Norwich. On main line passenger trains Class 86s replaced Class 47s and assorted other classes of diesel. In terms of freight, although pairs of Class 86s and single Class 90s have been regular performers over the years, in an average 24-hour period the number of diesel-hauled freights exceeds the number of electrically hauled examples. On 20 April 2009, Nos 86621 and 86632 approach Cranes Lane at Kelvedon on train 4M88, the 08.49 Felixstowe to Crewe Basford Hall Freightliner intermodal service. *Anthony Guppy*

▼ On 11 December 2009 No 90041 had No 70006 'dead in train' as it passed George Hall at Ardleigh, between Manningtree and Colchester, on 4M81, the 07.34 Felixstowe to Garston (south-east of Liverpool) intermodal. The brand-new North American-built General Electric Class 70 had just spent a few days at Ipswich for crew and artisan familiarisation and was being returned to Crewe. *Anthony Guppy*

▲ Many years ago there was almost a procession of freight trains over the Standedge route but in recent years waste trains and the occasional coal train are all that move in the daylight hours, other than for the ubiquitous Class 185 DMUs. Descending from Standedge Tunnel and approaching Marsden on 8 July 2008 with 'Binliner' 6M07, the 11.05 Roxby to Pendleton containing Greater Manchester's rubbish in orange containers, is Freightliner's No 66561. *Author*

▼ This powerful impression of the modern freight scene features immaculate and attractive-liveried Freightliner Heavy Haul Class 66/6 No 66615, seen approaching Reading West in May 2005 with the strikingly uniform load comprising 6M91 11.00 Theale to Earle's Sidings empty cement tanks. These will return to Derbyshire via Southall, Wellingborough and Clay Cross. The Class 66/6 has a tractive effort that is some 14 per cent higher than a standard Class 66, but at the expense of 10mph on top speed. *Author*

▲ Arguably one of the great freight train watching locations in the UK is Peak Forest in the Derbyshire hills. Although the overall volume of traffic may not be particularly high the surroundings are delightful and semaphore signalling prevails. In May 2010, when it was thought (incorrectly) that BR British-built Class 60s may have only weeks of life left, there was excitement as No 60085 worked past the typical Midland Railway signalbox with 6F05, the 15.25 Tunstead to Oakley. Early in 2011 it was announced that there would be a refurbishment programme that would result in 20 'Super 60s' having an extended working life of up to ten years. *Author*

▼ The deep throb of the large eight-cylinder Mirrlees diesel engine reverberated across the River Mersey at Walton, south of Warrington, at 09.10 on 13 May 2010 as No 60010 powered away from Arpley Yard with 6Z67, the 07.48 Liverpool Bulk Terminal to Ratcliffe Power Station imported coal train. It was a super way to start a day's photography and great to record an all-EWS livery consist before the DB Schenker paint brushes were applied. *Author*

▲ Although the 'good old days' of British Rail are mourned by many the good news for the railfan has been the proliferation of liveries, albeit some of them very short-lived. While some new freight companies have survived others have failed, including Fastline Freight, a subsidiary of Jarvis that went into liquidation. The failure occurred only a short time after Class 66s had been secured by the company. On hire to Colas on 13 May 2010 was spotless No 66434, seen approaching Acton Grange Junction with 6C19, the 12.06 Chirk to Carlisle timber empties. *Author*

▼ There is a reasonable amount of daytime freight over the famous Shap Summit, much of it diesel hauled. One of the more interesting trains with a colourful locomotive livery is train 6J37 Carlisle to Chirk timber loads operated by the Colas company. Their distinctive yellow, orange and black locomotives photograph well and here, No 66843 is seen passing Greenholme on 11 May 2010. It is easy to get 'bowled' because these timber trains sometimes work over the Settle & Carlisle line. *Author*

▲ Yet another freight company that is rapidly expanding is GBRf, owned and operated by the First Group. The company has gained a foothold in many freight flows and it has expansion in mind; for example, in March 2011 the company announced its new 'InterhubGB' service between Barking and Trafford Park, Manchester. GBRf No 66717 is seen passing Burton Salmon Junction on 22 September 2009 with loaded coal to feed the insatiable appetites of Eggborough or Drax power stations. *Author*

▼ Who would ever have thought that having produced some 11,000 HAA type wagons, mostly for merry-go-round coal train usage and which for years were the 'latest thing' to hit the railfreight scene, that by 2010 this would be the last rake in service, the 50 tonners having been ousted by new high-capacity bogie wagons. Climbing Shap and passing Greenholme in rapidly deteriorating weather on 11 May 2010 is No 66178 with 6F51, the 08.01 Earle's Sidings to New Cumnock via Carlisle coal empties. *Author*

▲ In a wonderful scene that post-dates the creation of a Nationalised British railway network by more than 63 years and dramatically demonstrating the progress made since the days of an old wheezing steam engine on a loose-coupled branch goods, is this modern image of our privatised railway system. Whispering past Winnick Junction at speed with some 3,650hp on tap and with the Freightliner name emblazoned on every wagon as well as the locomotive, 'PowerHaul' General Electric Class 70 No 70002 heads for Chalmerston in Scotland with 4Z39, the 15.30 from Fiddler's Ferry power station. Like them or loathe them, the sight was impressive. *Author*

▼ With the exception of the Class 60s the North American influence on our UK goods and freight-carrying railways will be with us for many decades. Indeed, if after the creation of British Railways we had then bought tried and tested American products a substantial amount of taxpayers' money would probably have been saved. Millions upon millions of pounds were squandered on what turned out to be defective engineering and design, compounded by poor management decisions of likely future motive power trends.

Nevertheless, there were some UK successes that we can be proud of and at the end of the day BR did keep the wheels of UK industry moving, despite the many trials and tribulations, often intransigent unions and bucketloads of government interference. Passing beneath the Unilever complex at Warrington is the new privatised 'kid on the block' in the shape of No 70002. *Author*

INDEX